Take Bread:

Early Writings on
Political Violence

Mortar Press, 2026, Philadelphia, PA.

ISBN: 978-1-957112-20-6

Mortar
Press

Underpinnings, from Mortar Press:
Affordable, pocket-sized editions of urgent
radical literature that is out of print, hard to find,
and otherwise calling for redistribution. Free
digital copies available at mortarpress.com.

Take Bread:

Early Writings on
Political Violence

EMMA GOLDMAN

1893–1917

Underpinnings

CONTENTS

THE UNION SQUARE SPEECH, AUGUST 21 *

Men and women, do you not realize that the State is the worst enemy you have? It is a machine that crushes you in order to sustain the ruling class, your masters. Like naïve children you put your trust in your political leaders. You make it possible for them to creep into your confidence, only to have them betray you to the first bidder. But even where there is no direct betrayal, the labor politicians make common cause with your enemies to keep you in leash, to prevent your direct action.

The State is the pillar of capitalism, and it is ridiculous to expect any redress from it. Do you not see the stupidity of asking relief from Albany with immense wealth within a stone's throw from here? Fifth Avenue is laid in gold, every mansion is a citadel of money and power. Yet there you stand, a giant, starved and fettered, shorn of

---

* This speech was originally delivered to a crowd of thousands, at the height of a catastrophic economic depression; Goldman would be charged for "incitement to riot" and sentenced with a year of imprisonment. This version is drawn from her later recollections in *Living My Life* (New York: Alfred A. Knopf, 1931), 122–123.

his strength.

Cardinal Manning long ago proclaimed that "necessity knows no law" and that "the starving man has a right to a share of his neighbor's bread." Cardinal Manning was an ecclesiastic steeped in the traditions of the Church, which has always been on the side of the rich against the poor. But he had some humanity, and he knew that hunger is a compelling force.

You, too, will have to learn that you have a right to share your neighbors bread. Your neighbors—they have not only stolen your bread, but they are sapping your blood. They will go on robbing you, your children, and your children's children, unless you wake up, unless you become daring enough to demand your rights. Well, then, demonstrate before the palaces of the rich; demand work. If they do not give you work, demand bread. If they deny you both, take bread.

It is your sacred right!

Emma Goldman

WHAT I BELIEVE *

1908

"What I believe" has many times been the target of hack writers. Such blood-curdling and incoherent stories have been circulated about me, it is no wonder that the average human being has palpitation of the heart at the very mention of the name Emma Goldman. It is too bad that we no longer live in the times when witches were burned at the stake or tortured to drive the evil spirit out of them. For, indeed, Emma Goldman is a witch! True, she does not eat little children, but she does many worse things. She manufactures bombs and gambles in crowned heads. B-r-r-r!

Such is the impression the public has of myself and my beliefs. It is therefore very much to the credit of *The World* that it gives its readers at least an opportunity to learn what my beliefs really are.

The student of the history of progressive thought is well aware that every idea in its early stages has

* First printed in *New York World*, July 19, 1908; this version is from Emma Goldman, *What I Believe*, 2nd ed. (New York: Mother Earth Publishing Association, 1908).

been misrepresented, and the adherents of such ideas have been maligned and persecuted. One need not go back two thousand years to the time when those who believed in the gospel of Jesus were thrown into the arena or hunted into dungeons to realize how little great beliefs or earnest believers are understood. The history of progress is written in the blood of men and women who have dared to espouse an unpopular cause, as, for instance, the black man's right to his body, or woman's right to her soul. If, then, from time immemorial, the New has met with opposition and condemnation, why should my beliefs be exempt from a crown of thorns?

"What I believe" is a process rather than a finality. Finalities are for gods and governments, not for the human intellect. While it may be true that Herbert Spencer's formulation of liberty is the most important on the subject, as a political basis of society, yet life is something more than formulas. In the battle for freedom, as Ibsen has so well pointed out, it is the *struggle* for, not so much the attainment of, liberty, that develops all that is strongest, sturdiest and finest in human character.

Anarchism is not only a process, however, that marches on with "somber steps," coloring all that is positive and constructive in organic development. It is a conspicuous protest of the most militant type. It is so absolutely uncompromising, insisting and permeating a force as to overcome the most stubborn assault and to withstand the criticism of those who really constitute the last trumpets of a decaying age.

Anarchists are by no means passive spectators in the theater of social development; on the contrary, they have some very positive notions as regards aims and methods.

That I may make myself as clear as possible without using too much space, permit me to adopt the topical mode of treatment of "What I Believe":

I. AS TO PROPERTY

"Property" means dominion over things and the denial to others of the use of those things. So long as production was not equal to the normal demand, institutional property may have had some *raison d'être*. One has only to consult economics, however, to know that the productivity of labor within the last few decades has increased so tremendously as to exceed normal demand a hundred-fold, and to make property not only a hindrance to human well-being, but an obstacle, a deadly barrier, to all progress. It is the private dominion over things that condemns millions of people to be mere nonentities, living corpses without originality or power of initiative, human machines of flesh and blood, who pile up mountains of wealth for others and pay for it with a gray, dull and wretched existence for themselves. I believe that there can be no real wealth, social wealth, so long as it rests on human lives—young lives, old lives and lives in the making.

It is conceded by all radical thinkers that the

fundamental cause of this terrible state of affairs is (1) that man must sell his labor; (2) that his inclination and judgment are subordinated to the will of a master.

Anarchism is the only philosophy that can and will do away with this humiliating and degrading situation. It differs from all other theories inasmuch as it points out that man's development, his physical well-being, his latent qualities and innate disposition alone must determine the character and conditions of his work. Similarly will one's physical and mental appreciations and his soul cravings decide how much he shall consume. To make this a reality will, I believe, be possible only in a society based on voluntary cooperation of productive groups, communities and societies loosely federated together, eventually developing into a free communism, actuated by a solidarity of interests. There can be no freedom in the large sense of the word, no harmonious development, so long as mercenary and commercial considerations play an important part in the determination of personal conduct.

II. AS TO GOVERNMENT

I believe government, organized authority, or the State is necessary *only* to maintain or protect property and monopoly. It has proven efficient in that function only. As a promoter of individual liberty, human well-being and social harmony, which alone constitute real order, government stands condemned by all the great men of the world.

I therefore believe, with my fellow-Anarchists, that the statutory regulations, legislative enactments, constitutional provisions, are invasive. They never yet induced man to do anything he could and would not do by virtue of his intellect or temperament, nor prevented anything that man was impelled to do by the same dictates. Millet's pictorial description of "The Man with the Hoe," Meunier's masterpieces of the miners that have aided in lifting labor from its degrading position, Gorki's descriptions of the underworld, Ibsen's psychological analysis of human life, could never have been induced by government any more than the spirit which impels a man to save a drowning child or a crippled woman from a burning building has ever been called into operation by statutory regulations or the policeman's club. I believe—indeed, I know—that whatever is fine and beautiful in the human expresses and asserts itself in spite of government, and not because of it.

The Anarchists are therefore justified in assuming that Anarchism—the absence of government—will insure the widest and greatest scope for unhampered human development, the cornerstone of true social progress and harmony.

As to the stereotyped argument that government acts as a check on crime and vise, even the makers of law no longer believe it. This country spends millions of dollars for the maintenance of her "criminals" behind prison bars, yet crime is on the increase. Surely this state of affairs is not owing to an insufficiency of laws! Ninety percent of all crimes are property crimes, which have their root in our economic iniquities. So long as these latter continue to exist we might convert every lamp-post into a gibbet without having the least effect on the crime in our midst. Crimes resulting from heredity can certainly never be cured by law. Surely we are learning even to-day that such crimes can effectively be treated only by the best modern medical methods at our command, and, above all, by the spirit of a deeper sense of fellowship, kindness and understanding.

III. AS TO MILITARISM

I should not treat of this subject separately, since it belongs to the paraphernalia of government, if it were not for the fact that those who are most vigorously opposed to my beliefs on the ground that the latter stand for force are the advocates of militarism.

The fact is that Anarchists are the only true advocates of peace, the only people who call a halt to the growing tendency of militarism, which is fast making of this erstwhile free country an imperialistic and despotic power.

The military spirit is the most merciless, heartless and brutal in existence. It fosters an institution for which there is not even a pretense of justification. The soldier, to quote Tolstoi, is a professional man-killer. He does not kill for the love of it, like a savage, or in a passion, like a homicide. He is a cold-blooded, mechanical, obedient tool of his military superiors. He is ready to cut throats or scuttle a ship at the command of his ranking officer, without knowing or, perhaps, caring how, why or wherefore. I am supported in this contention by no less a military light than Gen. Funston. I quote from the latter's communication to the New York *Evening Post* of June 30, dealing with the case of Private William Buwalda, which caused such a stir all through the Northwest. "The first duty of an officer or enlisted man," says our noble warrior, "is unquestioning obedience and loyalty to the government to which he has sworn allegiance; it makes no difference whether he approves of that government or not."

How can we harmonize the principle of "unquestioning obedience" with the principle of "life, liberty and the pursuit of happiness"? The deadly power of militarism has never before been so effectually demonstrated in this country as in the recent condemnation by court-martial of William Buwalda, of San Francisco, Company A, Engineers, to five years in military prison. Here was a man who had a record of fifteen years of continuous service. "His character and conduct were unimpeachable," we are told by Gen. Funston, who, in consideration of it, reduced Buwalda's sentence to three years. Yet the man is thrown suddenly out of the army, dishonored, robbed of his chances of a pension and sent to prison. What was his crime? Just listen, ye free-born Americans! William Buwalda attended a public meeting, and after the lecture he shook hands with the speaker. Gen. Funston, in his letter to the Post, to which I have already referred above, asserts that Buwalda's action was a "great military offense, infinitely worse than desertion." In another public statement, which the General made in Portland, Ore., he said that "Buwalda's was a serious crime, equal to treason."

It is quite true that the meeting had been arranged by Anarchists. Had the Socialists issued the call, Gen. Funston informs us, there would have been no objection to Buwalda's presence. Indeed, the General says, "I would not have the slightest hesitancy about attending a Socialist meeting myself." But to attend an Anarchist meeting with Emma Goldman as speaker—could there be anything more "treasonable"?

For this horrible crime a man, a free-born American citizen, who has given this country the best fifteen years of his life, and whose character and conduct during that time were "unimpeachable," is now languishing in a prison, dishonored, disgraced and robbed of a livelihood.

Can there be anything more destructive of the true genius of liberty than the spirit that made Buwalda's sentence possible—the spirit of unquestioning obedience? Is it for this that the American people have in the last few years sacrificed four hundred million dollars and their hearts' blood?

I believe that militarism—a standing army and navy in any country—is indicative of the decay of liberty and of the destruction of all that is best and finest in our nation.

The steadily growing clamor for more battleships and an increased army on the ground that these guarantee us peace is as absurd as the argument that the peaceful man is he who goes well armed.

The same lack of consistency is displayed by those peace pretenders who oppose Anarchism because it supposedly teaches violence, and who would yet be delighted over the possibility of the American nation soon being able to hurl dynamite bombs upon defenseless enemies from flying machines.

I believe that militarism will cease when the liberty-loving spirits of the world say to their masters: "Go and do your own killing. We have sacrificed ourselves and our loved ones long enough fighting your battles. In return you have made parasites and criminals of us in times of peace and brutalized us in times of war. You have separated us from our brothers and have made of the world a human slaughterhouse. No, we will not do your killing or fight for the country that you have stolen from us."

Oh, I believe with all my heart that human brotherhood and solidarity will clear the horizon from the terrible red streak of war and destruction.

IV. AS TO FREE SPEECH AND PRESS

The Buwalda case is only one phase of the larger question of free speech, free press and the right of free assembly.

Many good people imagine that the principles of free speech or press can be exercised properly and with safety within the limits of constitutional guarantees. That is the only excuse, it seems to me, for the terrible apathy and indifference to the onslaught upon free speech and press that we have witnessed in this county within the last few months.

I believe that free speech and press mean that I may say and write what I please. This right, when regulated by constitutional provisions, legislative enactments, almighty decisions of the Postmaster General or the policeman's club, becomes a farce. I am well aware that I will be warned of consequences if we remove the chains from speech and press. I believe, however, that the cure of consequences resulting from the unlimited exercise of expression is to allow more expression.

Mental shackles have never yet stemmed the tide of progress, whereas premature social explosions have only too often been brought about through a wave of repression.

Will our governors never learn that countries like England, Holland, Norway, Sweden and Denmark, with the largest freedom of expression, have been freest from "consequences"? Whereas Russia, Spain, Italy, France and, alas! even America, have raised these "consequences" to the most pressing political factor. Ours is supposed to be a country ruled by the majority, yet every policeman who is not vested with power by the majority can break up a meeting, drag the lecturer off the platform and club the audience out of the hall in true Russian fashion. The Postmaster General, who is not an elective officer, has the power to suppress publications and confiscate mail. From his decision there is no more appeal than from that of the Russian Czar. Truly, I believe we need a new Declaration of Independence. Is there no modern Jefferson or Adams?

V. AS TO THE CHURCH

At the recent convention of the political remnants of a once revolutionary idea it was voted that religion and vote getting have nothing to do with each other. Why should they? "So long as man is willing to delegate to the devil the care of his soul, he might, with the same consistency, delegate to the politician the care of his rights. That religion is a private affair has long been settled by the Bis-Marxian Socialists of Germany. Our American Marxians, poor of blood and originality, must needs go to Germany for their wisdom. That wisdom has served as a capital whip to lash the several millions of people into the well-disciplined army of Socialism. It might do the same here. For goodness' sake, let's not offend respectability, let's not hurt the religious feelings of the people.

Religion is a superstition that originated in man's mental inability to solve natural phenomena. The Church is an organized institution that has always been a stumbling block to progress.

Organized churchism has stripped religion of its

naïveté and primitiveness. It has turned religion into a nightmare that oppresses the human soul and holds the mind in bondage. "The Dominion of Darkness, as the last true Christian, Leo Tolstoi, calls the Church, has been a foe of human development and free thought, and as such it has no place in the life of a truly free people.

VI. AS TO MARRIAGE
AND LOVE

I believe these are probably the most tabooed subjects in this country. It is almost impossible to talk about them without scandalizing the cherished propriety of a lot of good folk. No wonder so much ignorance prevails relative to these questions. Nothing short of an open, frank, and intelligent discussion will purify the air from the hysterical, sentimental rubbish that is shrouding these vital subjects, vital to individual as well as social well-being.

Marriage and love are not synonymous; on the contrary, they are often antagonistic to each other. I am aware of the fact that some marriages are actuated by love, but the narrow, material confines of marriage, as it is, speedily crush the tender flower of affection.

Marriage is an institution which furnishes the State and Church with a tremendous revenue and the means of prying into that phase of life which refined people have long considered their own, their very own most sacred affair. Love is that most powerful factor of human relationship which from time immemorial has defied all man-made laws and broken through the iron bars of conventions in Church and morality. Marriage is often an economic arrangement purely, furnishing the woman with a lifelong life insurance policy and the man with a perpetuator of his kind or a pretty toy. That is, marriage, or the training thereto, prepares the woman for the life of a parasite, a dependent, helpless servant, while it furnishes the man the right of a chattel mortgage over a human life.

How can such a condition of affairs have anything in common with love?—with the element that would forego all the wealth of money and power and live in its own world of untrammeled human expression? But this is not the age of romanticism, of Romeo and Juliet, Faust and Marguerite, of moonlight ecstasies, of flowers and songs. Ours is a practical age. Our first consideration is an income. So much the worse for us if we have reached the era when the soul's highest flights are to be checked. No race can develop without the love element.

But if two people are to worship at the shrine of love, what is to become of the golden calf, marriage? "It is the only security for the woman, for the child, the family, the State." But it is no security to love; and without love no true home can or does exist. Without love no child should be born; without love no true woman can be related to a man. The fear that love is not sufficient material safety for the child is out of date. I believe when woman signs her own emancipation, her first declaration of independence will consist in admiring and loving a man for the qualities of his heart and mind and not for the quantities in his pocket. The second declaration will be that she has the right to follow that love without let or hindrance from the outside world. The third and most important declaration will be the absolute right to free motherhood.

In such a mother and an equally free father rests the safety of the child. They have the strength, the sturdiness, the harmony to create an atmosphere wherein alone the human plant can grow into an exquisite flower.

VII. AS TO ACTS OF VIOLENCE

And now I have come to that point in my beliefs about which the greatest misunderstanding prevails in the minds of the American public. "Well, come, now, don't you propagate violence, the killing of crowned heads and Presidents?" Who says that I do? Have you heard me, has anyone heard me? Has anyone seen it printed in our literature? No, but the papers say so, everybody says so; consequently it must be so. Oh, for the accuracy and logic of the dear public!

I believe that Anarchism is the only philosophy of peace, the only theory of the social relationship that values human life above everything else. I know that some Anarchists have committed acts of violence, but it is the terrible economic inequality and great political injustice that prompt such acts, not Anarchism. Every institution to-day rests on violence; our very atmosphere is saturated with it. So long as such a state exists we might as well strive to stop the rush of Niagara as hope to do away with violence. I have already stated that countries with some measure of freedom of expression have had few or no acts of violence. What is the moral? Simply this: No act committed by an Anarchist has been for personal gain, aggrandizement or profit, but rather a conscious protest against some repressive, arbitrary, tyrannical measure from above.

President Carnot, of France, was killed by Caserio in response to Carnot's refusal to commute the death sentence of Vaillant, for whose life the entire literary, scientific and humanitarian world of France had pleaded.

Bresci went to Italy on his own money, earned in the silk weaving mills of Paterson, to call King Humbert to the bar of justice for his order to shoot defenseless women and children during a bread riot. Angelino executed Prime Minister Canovas for the latter's resurrection of the Spanish inquisition at Montjuich Prison. Alexander Berkman attempted the life of Henry C. Frick during the Homestead strike only because of his intense sympathy for the eleven strikers killed by Pinkertons and for the widows and orphans evicted by Frick from their wretched little homes that were owned by Mr. Carnegie.

Every one of these men not only made his reasons known to the world in spoken or written statements, showing the cause that led to his act, proving that the unbearable economic and political pressure, the suffering and despair of their fellow-men, women and children prompted the acts, and not the philosophy of Anarchism. They came openly, frankly and ready to stand the consequences, ready to give their own lives.

In diagnosing the true nature of our social disease I cannot condemn those who, through no fault of their own, are suffering from a wide-spread malady.

I do not believe that these acts can, or ever have been intended to, bring about the social reconstruction. That can only be done, first, by a broad and wide education as to man's place in society and his proper relation to his fellows; and, second, through example. By example I mean the actual living of a truth once recognized, not the mere theorizing of its life element. Lastly, and the most powerful weapon, is the conscious, intelligent, organized, economic protest of the masses through direct action and the general strike.

The general contention that Anarchists are opposed to organization, and hence stand for chaos, is absolutely groundless. True, we do not believe in the compulsory, arbitrary side of organization that would compel people of antagonistic tastes and interests into a body and hold them there by coercion. Organization as the result of natural blending of common interests, brought about through voluntary adhesion, Anarchists do not only not oppose, but believe in as the only possible basis of social life.

It is the harmony of organic growth which produces variety of color and form—the complete whole we admire in the flower. Analogously will the organized activity of free human beings endowed with the spirit of solidarity result in the perfection of social harmony—which is Anarchism. Indeed, only Anarchism makes non-authoritarian organization a reality, since it abolishes the existing antagonism between individuals and classes.

ANARCHISM: WHAT IT REALLY STANDS FOR*

Anarchy

Ever reviled, accursed, ne'er understood,
  Thou art the grisly terror of our age.
"Wreck of all order," cry the multitude,
  "Art thou, and war and murder's endless rage."
O, let them cry. To them that ne'er have striven
  The truth that lies behind a word to find,
To them the word's right meaning was not given.
  They shall continue blind among the blind.
But thou, O word, so clear, so strong, so pure,
  Thou sayest all which I for goal have taken.
I give thee to the future! Thine secure
  When each at least unto himself shall waken.
Comes it in sunshine? In the tempest's thrill?
  I cannot tell—but it the earth shall see!
I am an Anarchist! Wherefore I will
  Not rule, and also ruled I will not be!

John Henry Mackay

* From Emma Goldman, *Anarchism and Other Essays*, 3rd ed. (New York: Mother Earth Publishing Association, 1917), 53–74.

The history of human growth and development is at the same time the history of the terrible struggle of every new idea heralding the approach of a brighter dawn. In its tenacious hold on tradition, the Old has never hesitated to make use of the foulest and cruelest means to stay the advent of the New, in whatever form or period the latter may have asserted itself. Nor need we retrace our steps into the distant past to realize the enormity of opposition, difficulties, and hardships placed in the path of every progressive idea. The rack, the thumbscrew, and the knout are still with us; so are the convict's garb and the social wrath, all conspiring against the spirit that is serenely marching on.

Anarchism could not hope to escape the fate of all other ideas of innovation. Indeed, as the most revolutionary and uncompromising innovator, Anarchism must needs meet with the combined ignorance and venom of the world it aims to reconstruct.

To deal even remotely with all that is being said and done against Anarchism would necessitate the writing of a whole volume. I shall therefore meet only two of the principal objections. In so doing, I shall attempt to elucidate what Anarchism really stands for.

The strange phenomenon of the opposition to Anarchism is that it brings to light the relation between so-called intelligence and ignorance. And yet this is not so very strange when we consider the relativity of all things. The ignorant mass has in its favor that it makes no pretense of knowledge or tolerance. Acting, as it always does, by mere impulse, its reasons are like those of a child. "Why?" "Because." Yet the opposition of the uneducated to Anarchism deserves the same consideration as that of the intelligent man.

What, then, are the objections? First, Anarchism is impractical, though a beautiful ideal. Second, Anarchism stands for violence and destruction, hence it must be repudiated as vile and dangerous. Both the intelligent man and the ignorant mass judge not from a thorough knowledge of the subject, but either from hearsay or false interpretation.

A practical scheme, says Oscar Wilde, is either one already in existence, or a scheme that could be carried out under the existing conditions; but it is exactly the existing conditions that one objects to, and any scheme that could accept these conditions is wrong and foolish. The true criterion of the practical, therefore, is not whether the latter can keep intact the wrong or foolish; rather is it whether the scheme has vitality enough to leave the stagnant waters of the old, and build, as well as sustain, new life. In the light of this conception, Anarchism is indeed practical. More than any other idea, it is helping to do away with the wrong and foolish; more than any other idea, it is building and sustaining new life.

The emotions of the ignorant man are continuously kept at a pitch by the most blood-curdling stories about Anarchism. Not a thing too outrageous to be employed against this philosophy and its exponents. Therefore Anarchism represents to the unthinking what the proverbial bad man does to the child,–a black monster bent on swallowing everything; in short, destruction and violence.

Destruction and violence! How is the ordinary man to know that the most violent element in society is ignorance; that its power of destruction is the very thing Anarchism is combating? Nor is he aware that Anarchism, whose roots, as it were, are part of nature's forces, destroys, not healthful tissue, but parasitic growths that feed on the life's essence of society. It is merely clearing the soil from weeds and sagebrush, that it may eventually bear healthy fruit.

Someone has said that it requires less mental effort to condemn than to think. The widespread mental indolence, so prevalent in society, proves this to be only too true. Rather than to go to the bottom of any given idea, to examine into its origin and meaning, most people will either condemn it altogether, or rely on some superficial or prejudicial definition of non-essentials.

Anarchism urges man to think, to investigate, to analyze every proposition; but that the brain capacity of the average reader be not taxed too much, I also shall begin with a definition, and then elaborate on the latter.

ANARCHISM: The philosophy of a new social order based on liberty unrestricted by man-made law; the theory that all forms of government rest on violence, and are therefore wrong and harmful, as well as unnecessary.

The new social order rests, of course, on the materialistic basis of life; but while all Anarchists agree that the main evil today is an economic one, they maintain that the solution of that evil can be brought about only through the consideration of every phase of life,–individual, as well as the collective; the internal, as well as the external phases.

A thorough perusal of the history of human development will disclose two elements in bitter conflict with each other; elements that are only now beginning to be understood, not as foreign to each other, but as closely related and truly harmonious, if only placed in proper environment: the individual and social instincts. The individual and society have waged a relentless and bloody battle for ages, each striving for supremacy, because each was blind to the value and importance of the other. The individual and social instincts,–the one a most potent factor for individual endeavor, for growth, aspiration, self-realization; the other an equally potent factor for mutual helpfulness and social well-being.

The explanation of the storm raging within the individual, and between him and his surroundings, is not far to seek. The primitive man, unable to understand his being, much less the unity of all life, felt himself absolutely dependent on blind, hidden forces ever ready to mock and taunt him. Out of that attitude grew the religious concepts of man as a mere speck of dust dependent on superior powers on high, who can only be appeased by complete surrender. All the early sagas rest on that idea, which continues to be the *Leitmotiv* of the biblical tales dealing with the relation of man to God, to the State, to society. Again and again the same motif, *man is nothing, the powers are everything*. Thus Jehovah would only endure man on condition of complete surrender. Man can have all the glories of the earth, but he must not become conscious of himself. The State, society, and moral laws all sing the same refrain: Man can have all the glories of the earth, but he must not become conscious of himself.

Anarchism is the only philosophy which brings to man the consciousness of himself; which maintains that God, the State, and society are non-existent, that their promises are null and void, since they can be fulfilled only through man's subordination. Anarchism is therefore the teacher of the unity of life; not merely in nature, but in man. There is no conflict between the individual and the social instincts, any more than there is between the heart and the lungs: the one the receptacle of a precious life essence, the other the repository of the element that keeps the essence pure and strong. The individual is the heart of society, conserving the essence of social life; society is the lungs which are distributing the element to keep the life essence–that is, the individual–pure and strong.

"The one thing of value in the world," says Emerson, "is the active soul; this every man contains within him. The soul active sees absolute truth and utters truth and creates." In other words, the individual instinct is the thing of value in the world. It is the true soul that sees and creates the truth alive, out of which is to come a still greater truth, the re-born social soul.

Anarchism is the great liberator of man from the phantoms that have held him captive; it is the arbiter and pacifier of the two forces for individual and social harmony. To accomplish that unity, Anarchism has declared war on the pernicious influences which have so far prevented the harmonious blending of individual and social instincts, the individual and society.

Religion, the dominion of the human mind; Property, the dominion of human needs; and Government, the dominion of human conduct, represent the stronghold of man's enslavement and all the horrors it entails. Religion! How it dominates man's mind, how it humiliates and degrades his soul. God is everything, man is nothing, says religion. But out of that nothing God has created a kingdom so despotic, so tyrannical, so cruel, so terribly exacting that naught but gloom and tears and blood have ruled the world since gods began. Anarchism rouses man to rebellion against this black monster. Break your mental fetters, says Anarchism to man, for not until you think and judge for yourself will you get rid of the dominion of darkness, the greatest obstacle to all progress.

Property, the dominion of man's needs, the denial of the right to satisfy his needs. Time was when property claimed a divine right, when it came to man with the same refrain, even as religion, "Sacrifice! Abnegate! Submit!" The spirit of Anarchism has lifted man from his prostrate position. He now stands erect, with his face toward the light. He has learned to see the insatiable, devouring, devastating nature of property, and he is preparing to strike the monster dead.

"Property is robbery," said the great French Anarchist Proudhon. Yes, but without risk and danger to the robber. Monopolizing the accumulated efforts of man, property has robbed him of his birthright, and has turned him loose a pauper and an outcast. Property has not even the time-worn excuse that man does not create enough to satisfy all needs. The A-B-C student of economics knows that the productivity of labor within the last few decades far exceeds normal demand. But what are normal demands to an abnormal institution? The only demand that property recognizes is its own gluttonous appetite for greater wealth, because wealth means power; the power to subdue, to crush, to exploit, the power to enslave, to outrage, to degrade. America is particularly boastful of her great power, her enormous national wealth. Poor America, of what avail is all her wealth, if the individuals comprising the nation are wretchedly poor? If they live in squalor, in filth, in crime, with hope and joy gone, a homeless, soilless army of human prey.

It is generally conceded that unless the returns of any business venture exceed the cost, bankruptcy is inevitable. But those engaged in the business of producing wealth have not yet learned even this simple lesson. Every year the cost of production in human life is growing larger (50,000 killed, 100,000 wounded in America last year); the returns to the masses, who help to create wealth, are ever getting smaller. Yet America continues to be blind to the inevitable bankruptcy of our business of production. Nor is this the only crime of the latter. Still more fatal is the crime of turning the producer into a mere particle of a machine, with less will and decision than his master of steel and iron. Man is being robbed not merely of the products of his labor, but of the power of free initiative, of originality, and the interest in, or desire for, the things he is making.

Real wealth consists in things of utility and beauty, in things that help to create strong, beautiful bodies and surroundings inspiring to live in. But if man is doomed to wind cotton around a spool, or dig coal, or build roads for thirty years of his life, there can be no talk of wealth. What he gives to the world is only gray and hideous things, reflecting a dull and hideous existence,–too weak to live, too cowardly to die. Strange to say, there are people who extol this deadening method of centralized production as the proudest achievement of our age. They fail utterly to realize that if we are to continue in machine subserviency, our slavery is more complete than was our bondage to the King. They do not want to know that centralization is not only the death-knell of liberty, but also of health and beauty, of art and science, all these being impossible in a clock-like, mechanical atmosphere.

Anarchism cannot but repudiate such a method of production: its goal is the freest possible expression of all the latent powers of the individual. Oscar Wilde defines a perfect personality as "one who develops under perfect conditions, who is not wounded, maimed, or in danger." A perfect personality, then, is only possible in a state of society where man is free to choose the mode of work, the conditions of work, and the freedom to work. One to whom the making of a table, the building of a house, or the tilling of the soil, is what the painting is to the artist and the discovery to the scientist,–the result of inspiration, of intense longing, and deep interest in work as a creative force. That being the ideal of Anarchism, its economic arrangements must consist of voluntary productive and distributive associations, gradually developing into free communism, as the best means of producing with the least waste of human energy. Anarchism, however, also recognizes the right of the individual, or numbers of individuals, to arrange at all times for other forms of work, in harmony with their tastes and desires.

Such free display of human energy being possible only under complete individual and social freedom, Anarchism directs its forces against the third and greatest foe of all social equality; namely, the State, organized authority, or statutory law,–the dominion of human conduct.

Just as religion has fettered the human mind, and as property, or the monopoly of things, has subdued and stifled man's needs, so has the State enslaved his spirit, dictating every phase of conduct. "All government in essence," says Emerson, "is tyranny." It matters not whether it is government by divine right or majority rule. In every instance its aim is the absolute subordination of the individual.

Referring to the American government, the greatest American Anarchist, David Thoreau, said: "Government, what is it but a tradition, though a recent one, endeavoring to transmit itself unimpaired to posterity, but each instance losing its integrity; it has not the vitality and force of a single living man. Law never made man a whit more just; and by means of their respect for it, even the well disposed are daily made agents of injustice."

Indeed, the keynote of government is injustice. With the arrogance and self-sufficiency of the King who could do no wrong, governments ordain, judge, condemn, and punish the most insignificant offenses, while maintaining themselves by the greatest of all offenses, the annihilation of individual liberty. Thus Ouida is right when she maintains that "the State only aims at instilling those qualities in its public by which its demands are obeyed, and its exchequer is filled. Its highest attainment is the reduction of mankind to clockwork. In its atmosphere all those finer and more delicate liberties, which require treatment and spacious expansion, inevitably dry up and perish. The State requires a taxpaying machine in which there is no hitch, an exchequer in which there is never a deficit, and a public, monotonous, obedient, colorless, spiritless, moving humbly like a flock of sheep along a straight high road between two walls."

Yet even a flock of sheep would resist the chicanery of the State, if it were not for the corruptive, tyrannical, and oppressive methods it employs to serve its purposes.

Therefore Bakunin repudiates the State as synonymous with the surrender of the liberty of the individual or small minorities,–the destruction of social relationship, the curtailment, or complete denial even, of life itself, for its own aggrandizement. The State is the altar of political freedom and, like the religious altar, it is maintained for the purpose of human sacrifice.

In fact, there is hardly a modern thinker who does not agree that government, organized authority, or the State, is necessary *only* to maintain or protect property and monopoly. It has proven efficient in that function only.

Even George Bernard Shaw, who hopes for the miraculous from the State under Fabianism, nevertheless admits that "it is at present a huge machine for robbing and slave-driving of the poor by brute force." This being the case, it is hard to see why the clever prefacer wishes to uphold the State after poverty shall have ceased to exist.

Unfortunately, there are still a number of people who continue in the fatal belief that government rests on natural laws, that it maintains social order and harmony, that it diminishes crime, and that it prevents the lazy man from fleecing his fellows. I shall therefore examine these contentions.

A natural law is that factor in man which asserts itself freely and spontaneously without any external force, in harmony with the requirements of nature. For instance, the demand for nutrition, for sex gratification, for light, air, and exercise, is a natural law. But its expression needs not the machinery of government, needs not the club, the gun, the handcuff, or the prison. To obey such laws, if we may call it obedience, requires only spontaneity and free opportunity. That governments do not maintain themselves through such harmonious factors is proven by the terrible array of violence, force, and coercion all governments use in order to live. Thus Blackstone is right when he says, "Human laws are invalid, because they are contrary to the laws of nature."

Unless it be the order of Warsaw after the slaughter of thousands of people, it is difficult to ascribe to governments any capacity for order or social harmony. Order derived through submission and maintained by terror is not much of a safe guaranty; yet that is the only "order" that governments have ever maintained. True social harmony grows naturally out of solidarity of interests. In a society where those who always work never have anything, while those who never work enjoy everything, solidarity of interests is non-existent; hence social harmony is but a myth. The only way organized authority meets this grave situation is by extending still greater privileges to those who have already monopolized the earth, and by still further enslaving the disinherited masses. Thus the entire arsenal of government–laws, police, soldiers, the courts, legislatures, prisons,–is strenuously engaged in "harmonizing" the most antagonistic elements in society.

The most absurd apology for authority and law is that they serve to diminish crime. Aside from the fact that the

State is itself the greatest criminal, breaking every written and natural law, stealing in the form of taxes, killing in the form of war and capital punishment, it has come to an absolute standstill in coping with crime. It has failed utterly to destroy or even minimize the horrible scourge of its own creation.

Crime is naught but misdirected energy. So long as every institution of today, economic, political, social, and moral, conspires to misdirect human energy into wrong channels; so long as most people are out of place doing the things they hate to do, living a life they loathe to live, crime will be inevitable, and all the laws on the statutes can only increase, but never do away with, crime. What does society, as it exists today, know of the process of despair, the poverty, the horrors, the fearful struggle the human soul must pass on its way to crime and degradation. Who that knows this terrible process can fail to see the truth in these words of Peter Kropotkin:

"Those who will hold the balance between the benefits thus attributed to law and punishment and the degrading effect of the latter on humanity; those who will estimate the torrent of depravity poured abroad in human society by the informer, favored by the Judge even, and paid for in clinking cash by governments, under the pretext of aiding to unmask crime; those who will go within prison walls and there see what human beings become when deprived of liberty, when subjected to the care of brutal keepers, to coarse, cruel words, to a thousand stinging, piercing humiliations, will agree with us that the entire apparatus of prison and punishment is an abomination which ought to be brought to an end."

The deterrent influence of law on the lazy man is too absurd to merit consideration. If society were only relieved of the waste and expense of keeping a lazy class, and the equally great expense of the paraphernalia of protection this lazy class requires, the social tables would contain an abundance for all, including even the occasional lazy individual. Besides, it is well to consider that laziness results either from special privileges, or physical and mental abnormalities. Our present insane system of production fosters both, and the most astounding phenomenon is that people should want to work at all now. Anarchism aims to strip labor of its deadening, dulling aspect, of its gloom and compulsion. It aims to make work an instrument of joy, of strength, of color, of real harmony, so that the poorest sort of a man should find in work both recreation and hope.

To achieve such an arrangement of life, government, with its unjust, arbitrary, repressive measures, must be done away with. At best it has but imposed one single mode of life upon all, without regard to individual and social variations and needs. In destroying government and statutory laws, Anarchism proposes to rescue the self-respect and independence of the individual from all restraint and invasion by authority. Only in freedom can man grow to his full stature. Only in freedom will he learn to think and move, and give the very best in him. Only in freedom will he realize the true force of the social bonds which knit men together, and which are the true foundation of a normal social life.

But what about human nature? Can it be changed? And if not, will it endure under Anarchism?

Poor human nature, what horrible crimes have been committed in thy name! Every fool, from king to policeman, from the flatheaded parson to the visionless dabbler in science, presumes to speak authoritatively of human nature. The greater the mental charlatan, the more definite his insistence on the wickedness and weaknesses of human nature. Yet, how can any one speak of it today, with every soul in a prison, with every heart fettered, wounded, and maimed?

John Burroughs has stated that experimental study of animals in captivity is absolutely useless. Their character, their habits, their appetites undergo a complete transformation when torn from their soil in field and forest. With human nature caged in a narrow space, whipped daily into submission, how can we speak of its potentialities?

Freedom, expansion, opportunity, and, above all, peace and repose, alone can teach us the real dominant factors of human nature and all its wonderful possibilities.

Anarchism, then, really stands for the liberation of the human mind from the dominion of religion; the liberation of the human body from the dominion of property; liberation from the shackles and restraint of government. Anarchism stands for a social order based on the free grouping of individuals for the purpose of producing real social wealth; an order that will guarantee to every human being free access to the earth and full enjoyment of the necessities of life, according to individual desires, tastes, and inclinations.

This is not a wild fancy or an aberration of the mind. It is the conclusion arrived at by hosts of intellectual men and women the world over; a conclusion resulting from the close and studious observation of the tendencies of modern society: individual liberty and economic equality, the twin forces for the birth of what is fine and true in man.

As to methods. Anarchism is not, as some may suppose, a theory of the future to be realized through divine inspiration. It is a living force in the affairs of our life, constantly creating new conditions. The methods of Anarchism therefore do not comprise an iron-clad program to be carried out under all circumstances. Methods must grow out of the economic needs of each place and clime, and of the intellectual and temperamental requirements of the individual. The serene, calm character of a Tolstoy will wish different methods for social reconstruction than the intense, overflowing personality of a Michael Bakunin or a Peter Kropotkin. Equally so it must be apparent that the economic and political needs of Russia will dictate more drastic measures than would England or America. Anarchism does not stand for military drill and uniformity; it does, however, stand for the spirit of revolt, in whatever form, against everything that hinders human growth. All Anarchists agree in that, as they also agree in their opposition to the political machinery as a means of bringing about the great social change.

"All voting," says Thoreau, "is a sort of gaming, like checkers, or backgammon, a playing with right and wrong; its obligation never exceeds that of expediency. Even voting for the right thing is doing nothing for it. A wise man will not leave the right to the mercy of chance, nor wish it to prevail through the power of the majority." A close examination of the machinery of politics and its achievements will bear out the logic of Thoreau.

What does the history of parliamentarism show? Nothing but failure and defeat, not even a single reform to ameliorate the economic and social stress of the people. Laws have been passed and enactments made for the improvement and protection of labor. Thus it was proven only last year that Illinois, with the most rigid laws for mine protection, had the greatest mine disasters. In States where child labor laws prevail, child exploitation is at its highest, and though with us the workers enjoy full political opportunities, capitalism has reached the most brazen zenith.

Even were the workers able to have their own representatives, for which our good Socialist politicians are clamoring, what chances are there for their honesty and good faith? One has but to bear in mind the process of politics to realize that its path of good intentions is full of pitfalls: wire-pulling, intriguing, flattering, lying, cheating; in fact, chicanery of every description, whereby the political aspirant can achieve success. Added to that is a complete demoralization of character and conviction, until nothing is left that would make one hope for anything from such a human derelict. Time and time again the people were foolish enough to trust, believe, and support with their last farthing aspiring politicians, only to find themselves betrayed and cheated.

It may be claimed that men of integrity would not become corrupt in the political grinding mill. Perhaps not; but such men would be absolutely helpless to exert the slightest influence in behalf of labor, as indeed has been shown in numerous instances. The State is the economic master of its servants. Good men, if such there be, would either remain true to their political faith and lose their economic support, or they would cling to their economic master and be utterly unable to do the slightest good. The political arena leaves one no alternative, one must either be a dunce or a rogue.

The political superstition is still holding sway over the hearts and minds of the masses, but the true lovers of liberty will have no more to do with it. Instead, they believe with Stirner that man has as much liberty as he is willing to take. Anarchism therefore stands for direct action, the open defiance of, and resistance to, all laws and restrictions, economic, social, and moral. But defiance and resistance are illegal. Therein lies the salvation of man. Everything illegal necessitates integrity, self-reliance, and courage. In short, it calls for free, independent spirits, for "men who are men, and who have a bone in their backs which you cannot pass your hand through."

Universal suffrage itself owes its existence to direct action. If not for the spirit of rebellion, of the defiance on the part of the American revolutionary fathers, their posterity would still wear the King's coat. If not for the direct action of a John Brown and his comrades, America would still trade in the flesh of the black man. True, the trade in white flesh is still going on; but that, too, will have to be abolished by direct action. Trade-unionism, the economic arena of the modern gladiator, owes its existence to direct action. It is but recently that law and government have attempted to crush the trade-union movement, and condemned the exponents of man's right to organize to prison as conspirators. Had they sought to assert their cause through begging, pleading, and compromise, trade-unionism would today be a negligible quantity. In France, in Spain, in Italy, in Russia, nay even in England (witness the growing rebellion of English labor unions), direct, revolutionary, economic action has become so strong a force in the battle for industrial liberty as to make the world realize the tremendous importance of labor's power. The General Strike, the supreme expression of the economic consciousness of the workers, was ridiculed in America but a short time ago. Today every great strike, in order to win, must realize the importance of the solidaric general protest.

Direct action, having proven effective along economic lines, is equally potent in the environment of the individual. There a hundred forces encroach upon his being, and only persistent resistance to them will finally set him free. Direct action against the authority in the shop, direct action against the authority of the law, direct action against the invasive, meddlesome authority of our moral code, is the logical, consistent method of Anarchism.

Will it not lead to a revolution? Indeed, it will. No real social change has ever come about without a revolution. People are either not familiar with their history, or they have not yet learned that revolution is but thought carried into action.

Anarchism, the great leaven of thought, is today permeating every phase of human endeavor. Science, art, literature, the drama, the effort for economic betterment, in fact every individual and social opposition to the existing disorder of things, is illumined by the spiritual light of Anarchism. It is the philosophy of the sovereignty of the individual. It is the theory of social harmony. It is the great, surging, living truth that is reconstructing the world, and that will usher in the Dawn.

THE POWER OF THE IDEAL*

> The man I touch, there awakens in his blood a burning fever, that shall lick his blood as fire. The fever that I will give him shall be cured when his life is cured.
>
> Olive Schreiner, in "A Dream of Wild Bees."

Twenty years ago the Power of the Ideal touched my soul, and there awakened a burning fever. I thought then that the cure is the most desirable thing in all the world, the thing one must strive for, the thing so close at hand.

Since then I have learned that the inexorable, implacable Power of the Ideal concerns itself not with the cure; that it is itself the cure, that shall lick your blood like fire. This, too, I have come to know, that he who will be cured

---

* Goldman published this essay short months after union organizer McNamara brothers pled guilty to bombing the *Los Angeles Times* building, killing 21 and injuring 100. At the time, L.A. was an anti-labor bastion and the *Times* was the mouthpiece of its robber barons; this direct action culminated a years-long national dynamiting campaign by the International Association of Bridge and Structural Iron Workers. From *Mother Earth* 7, no. 1 (March 1912): 24–27.

must forswear the Ideal. Never again shall the fierce, inspiring light lure him to its lofty heights; never again shall he know the longing for the thing that awakened him. to life. Such is the fate of him who has forsworn the Ideal.

Twenty years play but a small part in the eternity of time; yet in the face of disheartening, discouraging, and paralizing events, twenty years themselves are an eternity. But once the fever is awakened, time and space become obliterated, blood and tears are wiped out, all pain and sorrow put to naught, by the compelling Power of the Ideal.

For a brief period it seemed almost as if American labor had been touched by the magic hand, as if its soul had been born to life with the burning fever to lick its blood as fire. But it was a false alarm, a mere symptom mistaken for the real thing. The danger is now safely locked away behind the iron bars of St. Quentin prison, and American labor has fallen back into its usual state of mental inertia and spiritual apathy. They saw in the McNamaras merely the cure; but to the force that consumed the two brothers as with the burning fever, the American workers remained blind and indifferent.

Thus the truism has again proven itself that they who aim but for the cure are doomed to die. It matters not of what nature the cure: it is never aught but a drug, never aught but an apology for the dying fires of the ideal, too weak to kindle into life the burning fever that shall lick one's blood as fire.

Nowhere is this truism borne out with greater force than among those who pass as Socialists to-day. Time was when they were awake with a burning fever, when the illuminating light on the mountain top drew them on with impelling force. But that time is no more. Instead, the Socialists are now content with the cure,—the most dangerous of all cures, the politic cure, which has drugged their ideal to sleep, and completely extinguished the fever within them.

In Cleveland and Lorain, in Elyria and Columbus, in Dayton and Indianapolis, in St. Louis and Chicago, the political quacks are busy concocting the pills that are to bring the cure. Woe be to him or her who refuses the proscribed dose! They are anathema, and must be stoned to death. Like the Catholic Church, the Socialist machine has become the relentless, blind foe of the Ideal.

In Cleveland the machine dictates who of its members may be permitted to face the heathen Anarchist in public debate. In Lorain and Elyria, in Columbus, Indianapolis, and St. Louis, the same machine proclaims the ban on those who will not be cured by the political quacks. But the place that has proved most conclusively that the Socialists in their mad clamor for the cure have lost their ideal, is Dayton, O.

Perhaps our readers had better judge for themselves, that they may fully realize what the political zealots are doing in the name of the burning fever that once licked the soul of Socialism as a fire. In Dayton, O., the following resolution and statement were adopted antagonizing the scheduled debate for Sunday between Emma Goldman, the Anarchist, and Frank Midney:

> Resolved, That Local Dayton disapproves of any of its members debating with Miss Emma Goldman at this time, and hereby forbids such action on the part of any member.
>
> Resolved, That we authorize and instruct our recording secretary to secure a competent person or persons to attend the Goldman debate, if it should be held, in order to accurately report the same to the local; but that outside the person or persons so chosen by the recording secretary, Local Dayton requests the Socialists to remain away from the proposed debate.

Following is in part the statement prepared for the press:

> The Socialist Party has reached the stage of its constructive work. Our ultimate object is to take over the collectively used means of life and conduct them democratically for all the workers, and so for all the human race. And our method is just as fully determined as our ultimate object. We propose to accomplish our work by patiently and persistently building a political organization of and by the workers, which organization shall at last secure the entire power of government. We work entirely in the open. We are opposed to intrigue and individual action. We seek the intelligent and collective action of all the workers.

We are therefore opposed to Anarchy in all of its forms. But we are especially opposed to the Anarchists who are in power, the Anarchists of corrupt government and corrupt business. These are the opposition to our cause, and we seek to meet them in the open and defeat them.

We would have taken no notice of Miss Goldman's visit to this city if the public had not been imposed upon. The Socialists of Dayton are not debating with Miss Goldman at this time. We ask all Socialists of this city (organized and unorganized) to remain away from the proposed debate if it is held. The Socialists will not be represented should the debate occur.

All members of Local Dayton *are expressly forbidden to take any public part in the proposed event*.

We warn the public in advance that if any "Socialist" demonstration or opposition is reported to have occurred at the debate, if held, it will be a demonstration of Anarchists masquerading as Socialists. The answer of the Socialists will be to remain away from the proposed occasion. If the general public is interested in knowing the authorized word of the Socialists of Dayton with reference to the alleged dynamiters, they are cordially invited to attend a free meeting at the Auditorium Theatre, Sunday night, where that subject will be discussed.

The sinner has since been excommunicated from the

Socialist party, for a period of two years. Luckily this new church lacks the power to erect its scaffolds, or Mr. Midney would meet with the fate of the heretics of the past. It is to be hoped, for his sake, that he may see the terrible danger of this growing inquisition which would, if it could, become the modern Torquemada, yet more cruel, because lacking even the vision of the Spanish predecessor. Such is the penalty for those who mistake the cure for the ideal. A cure indeed, from its own life-dream, its own inspiring purpose, its own idealism, even. A cringing, creeping, nauseating thing, is this cure.

It seems dark just now on the horizon of American life; yet there is a glimmering light in the distance, calling and comforting to him who can but see it. Lawrence, Mass., is that light,—and the burning fever its newly awakened, impelling force. Thus the Ideal is never to be eradicated.

My meetings, though small, have made up the lack of numbers by interest and enthusiasm for the light that streams from Lawrence. Everywhere this light is giving birth to new hopes, to a new chord in the great human struggle. Never once have I appealed in vain in behalf of Lawrence, the battle ground where the great fight is being waged so heroically. If, then, my work had accomplished nothing else, the help for Lawrence would surely justify the pain the tour entails.

"And the burning fever I shall give him shall not be cured until life is cured." But life creates life; it therefore recreates the fever that shall lick the blood as fire. Such is the inexorable, implacable Power of the Ideal.

THE PSYCHOLOGY OF POLITICAL VIOLENCE*

To analyze the psychology of political violence is not only extremely difficult, but also very dangerous. If such acts are treated with understanding, one is immediately accused of eulogizing them. If, on the other hand, human sympathy is expressed with the *Attentäter*,[1] one risks being considered a possible accomplice. Yet it is only intelligence and sympathy that can bring us closer to the source of human suffering, and teach us the ultimate way out of it.

The primitive man, ignorant of natural forces, dreaded their approach, hiding from the perils they threatened. As man learned to understand Nature's phenomena, he realized that though these may destroy life and cause great loss, they also bring relief. To the earnest student it must be apparent that the accumulated forces in our

---

* This essay collects and refines over a decade of Goldman's writings on the topic, ranging from at least as far back as her 1901 "The Tragedy at Buffalo," on Leon Czolgosz. This version is from Emma Goldman, *Anarchism and Other Essays*, 85-114.

social and economic life, culminating in a political act of violence, are similar to the terrors of the atmosphere, manifested in storm and lightning.

To thoroughly appreciate the truth of this view, one must feel intensely the indignity of our social wrongs; one's very being must throb with the pain, the sorrow, the despair millions of people are daily made to endure. Indeed, unless we have become a part of humanity, we cannot even faintly understand the just indignation that accumulates in a human soul, the burning, surging passion that makes the storm inevitable.

The ignorant mass looks upon the man who makes a violent protest against our social and economic iniquities as upon a wild beast, a cruel, heartless monster, whose joy it is to destroy life and bathe in blood; or at best, as upon an irresponsible lunatic. Yet nothing is further from the truth. As a matter of fact, those who have studied the character and personality of these men, or who have come in close contact with them, are agreed that it is their supersensitiveness to the wrong and injustice surrounding them which compels them to pay the toll of our social crimes. The most noted writers and poets, discussing the psychology of political offenders, have paid them the highest tribute. Could anyone assume that these men had advised violence, or even approved of the acts? Certainly not. Theirs was the attitude of the social student, of the man who knows that beyond every violent act there is a vital cause.

Björnstjerne Björnson, in the second part of *Beyond*

Emma Goldman

Human Power, emphasizes the fact that it is among the Anarchists that we must look for the modern martyrs who pay for their faith with their blood, and who welcome death with a smile, because they believe, as truly as Christ did, that their martyrdom will redeem humanity.

François Coppée, the French novelist, thus expresses himself regarding the psychology of the *Attentäter*:

The reading of the details of Vaillant's execution left me in a thoughtful mood. I imagined him expanding his chest under the ropes, marching with firm step, stiffening his will, concentrating all his energy, and, with eyes fixed upon the knife, hurling finally at society his cry of malediction. And, in spite of me, another spectacle rose suddenly before my mind. I saw a group of men and women pressing against each other in the middle of the oblong arena of the circus, under the gaze of thousands of eyes, while from all the steps of the immense amphitheatre went up the terrible cry, *Ad leones!* and, below, the opening cages of the wild beasts.

I did not believe the execution would take place. In the first place, no victim had been struck with death, and it had long been the custom not to punish an abortive crime with the last degree of severity. Then, this crime, however terrible in intention, was disinterested, born of an abstract idea. The man's past, his abandoned childhood, his life of hardship, pleaded also in his favor. In the independent press generous voices were raised in his behalf, very loud and eloquent. 'A purely literary current of opinion' some have said, with no little scorn. *It is, on the contrary, an honor to the men of art and thought to have expressed once more their disgust at the scaffold.*

Again Zola, in *Germinal* and *Paris*, describes the tenderness and kindness, the deep sympathy with human suffering, of these men who close the chapter of their lives with a violent outbreak against our system.

Last, but not least, the man who probably better than anyone else understands the psychology of the Attentäter is M. Hamon, the author of the brilliant work *Une Psychologie du Militaire Professionnel*, who has arrived at these suggestive conclusions:

The positive method confirmed by the rational method enables us to establish an ideal type of Anarchist, whose mentality is the aggregate of common psychic characteristics. Every Anarchist partakes sufficiently of this ideal type to make it possible to differentiate him from other men. The typical Anarchist, then, may be defined as follows: A man perceptible by the spirit of revolt under one or more of its forms—opposition, investigation, criticism, innovation—endowed with a strong love of liberty, egoistic or individualistic, and possessed of great curiosity, a keen desire to know. These traits are supplemented by an ardent love of others, a highly developed moral sensitiveness, a profound sentiment of justice, and imbued with missionary zeal.

To the above characteristics, says Alvin F. Sanborn, must be added these sterling qualities: a rare love of animals, surpassing sweetness in all the ordinary relations of life, exceptional sobriety of demeanor, frugality and regularity, austerity, even, of living, and courage beyond compare.[2]

There is a truism that the man in the street seems always to forget, when he is abusing the Anarchists, or whatever party happens to be his *bête noire* for the moment, as the cause of some outrage just perpetrated. This indisputable fact is that homicidal outrages have, from time immemorial, been the reply of goaded and desperate classes, and goaded and desperate individuals, to wrongs from their fellowmen, which they felt to be intolerable. Such acts are the violent recoil from violence, whether aggressive or repressive; they are the last desperate struggle of outraged and exasperated human nature for breathing space and life. And their cause lies not in any special conviction, but in the depths of that human nature itself. The whole course of history, political and social, is strewn with evidence of this fact. To go no further, take the three most notorious examples of political parties goaded into violence during the last fifty years: the Mazzinians in Italy, the Fenians in Ireland, and the

Terrorists in Russia. Were these people Anarchists? No. Did they all three even hold the same political opinions? No. The Mazzinians were Republicans, the Fenians political separatists, the Russians Social Democrats or Constitutionalists. But all were driven by desperate circumstances into this terrible form of revolt. And when we turn from parties to individuals who have acted in like manner, we stand appalled by the number of human beings goaded and driven by sheer desperation into conduct obviously violently opposed to their social instincts.

Now that Anarchism has become a living force in society, such deeds have been sometimes committed by Anarchists, as well as by others. For no new faith, even the most essentially peaceable and humane the mind of man has yet accepted, but at its first coming has brought upon earth not peace, but a sword; not because of anything violent or anti-social in the doctrine itself; simply because of the ferment any new and creative idea excites in men's minds, whether they accept or reject it. And a conception of Anarchism, which, on one hand, threatens every vested interest, and, on the other, holds out a vision of a free and noble life to be won by a struggle against existing wrongs, is certain to rouse the fiercest opposition, and bring the whole repressive force of ancient evil into violent contact with the tumultuous outburst of a new hope.

Under miserable conditions of life, any vision of the possibility of better things makes the present misery more intolerable, and spurs those who suffer to the most energetic struggles to improve their lot, and if these struggles only immediately result in sharper misery, the outcome is sheer desperation. In our present society, for instance, an exploited wage worker, who catches a glimpse of what work and life might and ought to be, finds the toilsome routine and the squalor of his existence almost intolerable; and even when he has the resolution and courage to continue steadily working his best, and waiting until new ideas have so permeated society as to pave the way for better times, the mere fact that he has such ideas and tries to spread them, brings him into difficulties with his employers. How many thousands of Socialists, and above all Anarchists, have lost work and even the chance of work, solely on the ground of their opinions. It is only the specially gifted craftsman, who, if he be a zealous propagandist, can hope to retain permanent employment. And what happens to a man with his brain working actively with a ferment of new ideas, with a vision before his eyes of a new hope dawning for toiling and agonizing men, with the knowledge that his suffering and that of his fellows in misery is not caused by the cruelty of fate, but by the injustice of other human beings,—what happens to such a man when he sees those dear to him starving, when he himself is starved? Some natures in such a plight, and those by no means the least social or the least sensitive, will become violent, and will even feel that their violence is social and not anti-social, that in striking when and how they can, they are striking, not for themselves, but for human nature, outraged and despoiled in their persons and in those of their fellow sufferers. And are we, who ourselves are not in this horrible predicament, to stand by and coldly condemn these piteous victims of the Furies and Fates? Are we to decry as miscreants these human beings who act with heroic self-devotion, sacrificing their lives in protest, where less social and less energetic natures would lie down and grovel in abject submission to injustice and wrong? Are we to join the ignorant and brutal outcry which stigmatizes such men as monsters of wickedness, gratuitously running amuck in a harmonious and innocently peaceful society? No! We hate murder with a hatred that may seem absurdly exaggerated to apologists for Matabele massacres, to callous acquiescers in hangings and bombardments, but we decline in such cases of homicide, or attempted homicide, as those of which we are treating, to be guilty of the cruel injustice of flinging the whole responsibility of the deed upon the immediate perpetrator. The guilt of these homicides lies upon every man and woman who, intentionally or by cold indifference, helps to keep up social conditions that drive human beings to despair. The man who flings his whole life into the attempt, at the cost of his own life, to protest against the wrongs of his fellow men, is a saint compared to the active and passive upholders of cruelty and injustice, even

> if his protest destroy other lives besides his own. Let
> him who is without sin in society cast the first stone at
> such an one.[3]

That every act of political violence should nowadays be attributed to Anarchists is not at all surprising. Yet it is a fact known to almost everyone familiar with the Anarchist movement that a great number of acts, for which Anarchists had to suffer, either originated with the capitalist press or were instigated, if not directly perpetrated, by the police.

For a number of years acts of violence had been committed in Spain, for which the Anarchists were held responsible, hounded like wild beasts, and thrown into prison. Later it was disclosed that the perpetrators of these acts were not Anarchists, but members of the police department. The scandal became so widespread that the conservative Spanish papers demanded the apprehension and punishment of the gang-leader, Juan Rull, who was subsequently condemned to death and executed. The sensational evidence, brought to light during the trial, forced Police Inspector Momento to exonerate completely the Anarchists from any connection with the acts committed during a long period. This resulted in the dismissal of a number of police officials, among them Inspector Tressols, who, in revenge, disclosed the fact that behind the gang of police bomb throwers were others of far higher position, who provided them with funds and protected them.

This is one of the many striking examples of how Anarchist conspiracies are manufactured.

That the American police can perjure themselves with the same ease, that they are just as merciless, just as brutal and cunning as their European colleagues, has been proven on more than one occasion. We need only recall the tragedy of the eleventh of November, 1887, known as the Haymarket Riot.

No one who is at all familiar with the case can possibly doubt that the Anarchists, judicially murdered in Chicago, died as victims of a lying, blood-thirsty press and of a cruel police conspiracy. Has not Judge Gary himself said: "Not because you have caused the Haymarket bomb, but because you are Anarchists, you are on trial."

The impartial and thorough analysis by Governor Altgeld of that blotch on the American escutcheon verified the brutal frankness of Judge Gary. It was this that induced Altgeld to pardon the three Anarchists, thereby earning the lasting esteem of every liberty-loving man and woman in the world.

When we approach the tragedy of September sixth, 1901, we are confronted by one of the most striking examples of how little social theories are responsible for an act of political violence. "Leon Czolgosz, an Anarchist, incited to commit the act by Emma Goldman." To be sure, has she not incited violence even before her birth, and will she not continue to do so beyond death? Everything is possible with the Anarchists.

Today, even, nine years after the tragedy, after it was

proven a hundred times that Emma Goldman had nothing to do with the event, that no evidence whatsoever exists to indicate that Czolgosz ever called himself an Anarchist, we are confronted with the same lie, fabricated by the police and perpetuated by the press. No living soul ever heard Czolgosz make that statement, nor is there a single written word to prove that the boy ever breathed the accusation. Nothing but ignorance and insane hysteria, which have never yet been able to solve the simplest problem of cause and effect.

The President of a free Republic killed! What else can be the cause, except that the Attentäter must have been insane, or that he was incited to the act.

A free Republic! How a myth will maintain itself, how it will continue to deceive, to dupe, and blind even the comparatively intelligent to its monstrous absurdities. A free Republic! And yet within a little over thirty years a small band of parasites have successfully robbed the American people, and trampled upon the fundamental principles, laid down by the fathers of this country, guaranteeing to every man, woman, and child "life, liberty, and the pursuit of happiness." For thirty years they have been increasing their wealth and power at the expense of the vast mass of workers, thereby enlarging the army of the unemployed, the hungry, homeless, and friendless portion of humanity, who are tramping the country from east to west, from north to south, in a vain search for work. For many years the home has been left to the care of the little ones, while the parents are exhausting their life and strength for a mere pittance. For thirty years the sturdy sons of America have been sacrificed on the battlefield of industrial war, and the daughters outraged in corrupt factory surroundings. For long and weary years this process of undermining the nation's health, vigor, and pride, without much protest from the disinherited and oppressed, has been going on. Maddened by success and victory, the money powers of this "free land of ours" became more and more audacious in their heartless, cruel efforts to compete with the rotten and decayed European tyrannies for supremacy of power.

In vain did a lying press repudiate Leon Czolgosz as a foreigner. The boy was a product of our own free American soil, that lulled him to sleep with,

> My country, 'tis of thee,
> Sweet land of liberty.

Who can tell how many times this American child had gloried in the celebration of the Fourth of July, or of Decoration Day, when he faithfully honored the Nation's dead? Who knows but that he, too, was willing to "fight for his country and die for her liberty," until it dawned upon him that those he belonged to have no country, because they have been robbed of all that they have produced; until he realized that the liberty and independence of his youthful dreams were but a farce. Poor Leon Czolgosz, your crime consisted of too sensitive a social consciousness. Unlike your idealless and brainless American brothers, your ideals soared above the belly and the bank account. No wonder you impressed the one human being among all the infuriated mob at your trial—a newspaper woman—as a visionary, totally oblivious to your surroundings. Your large, dreamy eyes must have beheld a new and glorious dawn.

Now, to a recent instance of police-manufactured Anarchist plots. In that bloodstained city Chicago, the life of Chief of Police Shippy was attempted by a young man named Averbuch. Immediately the cry was sent to the four corners of the world that Averbuch was an Anarchist, and that Anarchists were responsible for the act. Everyone who was at all known to entertain Anarchist ideas was closely watched, a number of people arrested, the library of an Anarchist group confiscated, and all meetings made impossible. It goes without saying that, as on various previous occasions, I must needs be held responsible for the act. Evidently the American police credit me with occult powers. I did not know Averbuch; in fact, had never before heard his name, and the only way I could have possibly "conspired" with him was in my astral body. But, then, the police are not concerned with logic or justice. What they seek is a target, to mask their absolute ignorance of the cause, of the psychology of a political act. Was Averbuch an Anarchist? There is no positive proof of it. He had been but three months in the country, did not know the language, and, as far as I could ascertain, was quite unknown to the Anarchists of Chicago.

What led to his act? Averbuch, like most young Russian

immigrants, undoubtedly believed in the mythical liberty of America. He received his first baptism by the policeman's club during the brutal dispersement of the unemployed parade. He further experienced American equality and opportunity in the vain efforts to find an economic master. In short, a three months' sojourn in the glorious land brought him face to face with the fact that the disinherited are in the same position the world over. In his native land he probably learned that necessity knows no law—there was no difference between a Russian and an American policeman.

The question to the intelligent social student is not whether the acts of Czolgosz or Averbuch were practical, any more than whether the thunderstorm is practical. The thing that will inevitably impress itself on the thinking and feeling man and woman is that the sight of brutal clubbing of innocent victims in a so-called free Republic, and the degrading, soul-destroying economic struggle, furnish the spark that kindles the dynamic force in the overwrought, outraged souls of men like Czolgosz or Averbuch. No amount of persecution, of hounding, of repression, can stay this social phenomenon.

But, it is often asked, have not acknowledged Anarchists committed acts of violence? Certainly they have, always however ready to shoulder the responsibility. My contention is that they were impelled, not by the teachings of Anarchism, but by the tremendous pressure of conditions, making life unbearable to their sensitive natures. Obviously, Anarchism, or any other social theory, making man a conscious social unit, will act as a leaven for rebellion. This is not a mere assertion, but a fact verified by all experience. A close examination of the circumstances bearing upon this question will further clarify my position.

Let us consider some of the most important Anarchist acts within the last two decades. Strange as it may seem, one of the most significant deeds of political violence occurred here in America, in connection with the Homestead strike of 1892.

During that memorable time the Carnegie Steel Company organized a conspiracy to crush the Amalgamated Association of Iron and Steel Workers. Henry Clay Frick, then Chairman of the Company, was intrusted with that democratic task. He lost no time in carrying out the policy of breaking the Union, the policy which he had so successfully practiced during his reign of terror in the coke regions. Secretly, and while peace negotiations were being purposely prolonged, Frick supervised the military preparations, the fortification of the Homestead Steel Works, the erection of a high board fence, capped with barbed wire and provided with loopholes for sharpshooters. And then, in the dead of night, he attempted to smuggle his army of hired Pinkerton thugs into Homestead, which act precipitated the terrible carnage of the steel workers. Not content with the death of eleven victims, killed in the Pinkerton skirmish, Henry Clay Frick, good Christian and free American, straightway began the hounding down of the helpless wives and orphans, by ordering them out of the wretched Company houses.

The whole country was aroused over these inhuman outrages. Hundreds of voices were raised in protest, calling on Frick to desist, not to go too far. Yes, hundreds of people protested—as one objects to annoying flies. Only one there was who actively responded to the outrage at Homestead—Alexander Berkman. Yes, he was an Anarchist. He gloried in that fact, because it was the only force that made the discord between his spiritual longing and the world without at all bearable. Yet not Anarchism, as such, but the brutal slaughter of the eleven steel workers was the urge for Alexander Berkman's act, his attempt on the life of Henry Clay Frick.

The record of European acts of political violence affords numerous and striking instances of the influence of environment upon sensitive human beings.

The court speech of Vaillant, who, in 1894, exploded a bomb in the Paris Chamber of Deputies, strikes the true keynote of the psychology of such acts:

Gentlemen, in a few minutes you are to deal your blow, but in receiving your verdict I shall have at least the satisfaction of having wounded the existing society, that cursed society in which one may see a single man spending, uselessly, enough to feed thousands of families; an infamous society which permits a few individuals to monopolize all the social wealth, while there are hundreds of thousands of unfortunates who have not even the bread that is not refused to dogs, and while entire families are committing suicide for want of the necessities of life.

Ah, gentlemen, if the governing classes could go down among the unfortunates! But no, they prefer to remain deaf to their appeals. It seems that a fatality impels them, like the royalty of the eighteenth century, toward the precipice which will engulf them, for woe be to those who remain deaf to the cries of the starving, woe to those who, believing themselves of superior essence, assume the right to exploit those beneath them! There comes a time when the people no longer reason; they rise like a hurricane, and pass away like a torrent. Then we see bleeding heads impaled on pikes.

Among the exploited, gentlemen, there are two classes of individuals. Those of one class, not realizing what they are and what they might be, take life as it comes, believe that they are born to be slaves, and content themselves with the little that is given them in exchange for their labor. But there are others, on the contrary, who think, who study, and who, looking about them, discover social iniquities. Is it their fault if they see clearly and suffer at seeing others suffer? Then they throw themselves into the struggle, and make themselves the bearers of the popular claims.

Gentlemen, I am one of these last. Wherever I have gone, I have seen unfortunates bent beneath the yoke of capital. Everywhere I have seen the same wounds causing tears of blood to flow, even in the remoter parts of the inhabited districts of South America, where I had the right to believe that he who was weary of the pains of civilization might rest in the shade of the palm trees and there study nature. Well, there even, more than elsewhere, I have seen capital come, like a vampire, to suck the last drop of blood of the unfortunate pariahs.

Then I came back to France, where it was reserved for me to see my family suffer atrociously. This was the last drop in the cup of my sorrow. Tired of leading this life of suffering and cowardice, I carried this bomb to those who are primarily responsible for social misery.

I am reproached with the wounds of those who were hit by my projectiles. Permit me to point out in passing that, if the bourgeois had not massacred or caused massacres during the Revolution, it is probable that they would still be under the yoke of the nobility. On the other hand, figure up the dead and wounded on Tonquin, Madagascar, Dahomey, adding thereto the thousands, yes, millions of unfortunates who die in the factories, the mines, and wherever the grinding power of capital is felt. Add also those who die of hunger, and all this with the assent of our Deputies. Beside all this, of how little weight are the reproaches now brought against me!

It is true that one does not efface the other; but, after all, are we not acting on the defensive when we respond to the blows which we receive from above? I know very well that I shall be told that I ought to have confined myself to speech for the vindication of the people's claims. But what can you expect! It takes a loud voice to make the deaf hear. Too long have they answered our voices by imprisonment, the rope, rifle volleys. Make no mistake; the explosion of my bomb is not only the cry of the rebel Vaillant, but the cry of an entire class which vindicates its rights, and which will soon add acts to words. For, be sure of it, in vain will they pass laws. The ideas of the thinkers will not halt; just as, in the last century, all the governmental forces could not prevent the Diderots and the Voltaires from spreading emancipating ideas among the people, so all the existing governmental forces will not prevent the Reclus, the Darwins, the Spencers, the Ibsens, the Mirbeaus, from spreading the ideas of justice and liberty which will annihilate the prejudices that hold the mass in ignorance. And these ideas, welcomed by the unfortunate, will flower in acts of revolt as they have done in me, until the day when the disappearance of authority shall permit all men to organize freely according to their choice, when everyone shall be able to enjoy the product of his labor, and when those moral maladies called prejudices shall vanish, permitting human beings to live in harmony, having no other desire than to study the sciences and love their fellows.

I conclude, gentlemen, by saying that a society in which one sees such social inequalities as we see all about us, in which we see every day suicides caused by poverty, prostitution flaring at every street corner,—a society whose principal monuments are barracks and prisons,—such a society must be transformed as soon as possible, on pain of being eliminated, and that speedily, from the human race. Hail to him who labors, by no matter what means, for this transformation! It is this idea that has guided me in my duel with authority, but as in this duel I have only wounded my adversary, it is now its turn to strike me.

Now, gentlemen, to me it matters little what penalty you may inflict, for, looking at this assembly with the eyes of reason, I can not help smiling to see you, atoms lost in matter, and reasoning only because you possess a prolongation of the spinal marrow, assume the right to judge one of your fellows.

Ah! gentlemen, how little a thing is your assembly and your verdict in the history of humanity; and human history, in its turn, is likewise a very little thing in the whirlwind which bears it through immensity, and which is destined to disappear, or at least to be transformed, in order to begin again the same history and the same facts, a veritably perpetual play of cosmic forces renewing and transferring themselves forever.

Will anyone say that Vaillant was an ignorant, vicious man, or a lunatic? Was not his mind singularly clear and analytic? No wonder that the best intellectual forces of France spoke in his behalf, and signed the petition to President Carnot, asking him to commute Vaillant's death sentence.

Carnot would listen to no entreaty; he insisted on more than a pound of flesh, he wanted Vaillant's life, and then—the inevitable happened: President Carnot was killed. On the handle of the stiletto used by the Attentäter was engraved, significantly,

VAILLANT!

Santa Caserio was an Anarchist. He could have gotten away, saved himself; but he remained, he stood the consequences.

His reasons for the act are set forth in so simple, dignified, and childlike manner that one is reminded of the touching tribute paid Caserio by his teacher of the little village school, Ada Negri, the Italian poet, who spoke of him as a sweet, tender plant, of too fine and sensitive texture to stand the cruel strain of the world.

Gentlemen of the Jury! I do not propose to make a defense, but only an explanation of my deed.

Since my early youth I began to learn that present society is badly organized, so badly that every day many wretched men commit suicide, leaving women and children in the most terrible distress. Workers, by thousands, seek for work and can not find it. Poor families beg for food and shiver with cold; they suffer the greatest misery; the little ones ask their miserable mothers for food, and the mothers cannot give it to them, because they have nothing. The few things which the home contained have already been sold or pawned. All they can do is beg alms; often they are arrested as vagabonds.

I went away from my native place because I was frequently moved to tears at seeing little girls of eight or ten years obliged to work fifteen hours a day for the paltry pay of twenty centimes. Young women of eighteen or twenty also work fifteen hours daily, for a mockery of remuneration. And that happens not only to my fellow countrymen, but to all the workers, who sweat the whole day long for a crust of bread, while their labor produces wealth in abundance. The workers are obliged to live under the most wretched conditions, and their food consists of a little bread, a few spoonfuls of rice, and water; so by the time they are thirty or forty years old, they are exhausted, and go to die in the hospitals. Besides, in consequence of bad food and overwork, these unhappy creatures are, by hundreds, devoured by pellagra—a disease that, in my country, attacks, as the physicians say, those who are badly fed and lead a life of toil and privation.

I have observed that there are a great many people who are hungry, and many children who suffer, whilst bread and clothes abound in the towns. I saw many and large shops full of clothing and woolen stuffs, and I also saw warehouses full of wheat and Indian corn, suitable for those who are in want. And, on the other hand, I saw thousands of people who do not work, who produce nothing and live on the labor of others; who spend every day thousands of francs for their amusement; who debauch the daughters of the workers; who own dwellings of forty or fifty rooms; twenty or thirty horses, many servants; in a word, all the pleasures of life.

I believed in God; but when I saw so great an inequality between men, I acknowledged that it was not God who created man, but man who created God. And I discovered that those who want their property to be respected, have an interest in preaching the existence of paradise and hell, and in keeping the people in ignorance.

Not long ago, Vaillant threw a bomb in the Chamber of Deputies, to protest against the present system of society. He killed no one, only wounded some persons; yet bourgeois justice sentenced him to death. And not satisfied with the condemnation of the guilty man, they began to pursue the Anarchists, and arrest not only those who had known Vaillant, but even those who had merely been present at any Anarchist lecture.

The government did not think of their wives and children. It did not consider that the men kept in prison were not the only ones who suffered, and that their little ones cried for bread. Bourgeois justice did not trouble itself about these innocent ones, who do not yet know what society is. It is no fault of theirs that their fathers are in prison; they only want to eat.

The government went on searching private houses, opening private letters, forbidding lectures and meetings, and practicing the most infamous oppressions against us. Even now, hundreds of Anarchists are arrested for having written an article in a newspaper, or for having expressed an opinion in public.

Gentlemen of the Jury, you are representatives of bourgeois society. If you want my head, take it; but do not believe that in so doing you will stop the Anarchist propaganda. Take care, for men reap what they have sown.

During a religious procession in 1896, at Barcelona, a bomb was thrown. Immediately three hundred men and women were arrested. Some were Anarchists, but the majority were trade-unionists and Socialists. They were thrown into that terrible bastille Montjuich, and subjected to most horrible tortures. After a number had been killed, or had gone insane, their cases were taken up by the liberal press of Europe, resulting in the release of a few survivors.

The man primarily responsible for this revival of the Inquisition was Canovas del Castillo, Prime Minister of Spain. It was he who ordered the torturing of the victims, their flesh burned, their bones crushed, their tongues cut out. Practiced in the art of brutality during his régime in Cuba, Canovas remained absolutely deaf to the appeals and protests of the awakened civilized conscience.

In 1897 Canovas del Castillo was shot to death by a young Italian, Angiolillo. The latter was an editor in his native land, and his bold utterances soon attracted the attention of the authorities. Persecution began, and Angiolillo fled from Italy to Spain, thence to France and Belgium, finally settling in England. While there he found employment as a compositor, and immediately became the friend of all his colleagues. One of the latter thus described Angiolillo:

> His appearance suggested the journalist rather than the disciple of Guttenberg. His delicate hands, moreover, betrayed the fact that he had not grown up at the 'case.' With his handsome frank face, his soft dark hair, his alert expression, he looked the very type of the vivacious Southerner. Angiolillo spoke Italian, Spanish, and French, but no English; the little French I knew was not sufficient to carry on a prolonged conversation. However, Angiolillo soon began to acquire the English idiom; he learned rapidly, playfully, and it was not long until he became very popular with his fellow compositors. His distinguished and yet modest manner, and his consideration towards his colleagues, won him the hearts of all the boys.

Angiolillo soon became familiar with the detailed accounts in the press. He read of the great wave of human sympathy with the helpless victims at Montjuich. On Trafalgar Square he saw with his own eyes the results of those atrocities, when the few Spaniards, who escaped Castillo's clutches, came to seek asylum in England.

There, at the great meeting, these men opened their shirts and showed the horrible scars of burned flesh. Angiolillo saw, and the effect surpassed a thousand theories; the impetus was beyond words, beyond arguments, beyond himself even.

Señor Antonio Canovas del Castillo, Prime Minister of Spain, sojourned at Santa Agueda. As usual in such cases, all strangers were kept away from his exalted presence. One exception was made, however, in the case of a distinguished looking, elegantly dressed Italian—the representative, it was understood, of an important journal. The distinguished gentleman was—Angiolillo.

Señor Canovas, about to leave his house, stepped on the veranda. Suddenly Angiolillo confronted him. A shot rang out, and Canovas was a corpse.

The wife of the Prime Minister rushed upon the scene. "Murderer! Murderer!" she cried, pointing at Angiolillo. The latter bowed. "Pardon, Madame," he said, "I respect you as a lady, but I regret that you were the wife of that man."

Calmly Angiolillo faced death. Death in its most terrible form—for the man whose soul was as a child's.

He was garroted. His body lay, sun-kissed, till the day hid in twilight. And the people came, and pointing the finger of terror and fear, they said: "There—the criminal—the cruel murderer."

How stupid, how cruel is ignorance! It misunderstands always, condemns always.

A remarkable parallel to the case of Angiolillo is to be

found in the act of Gaetano Bresci, whose Attentat upon King Umberto made an American city famous.

Bresci came to this country, this land of opportunity, where one has but to try to meet with golden success. Yes, he too would try to succeed. He would work hard and faithfully. Work had no terrors for him, if it would only help him to independence, manhood, self-respect.

Thus full of hope and enthusiasm he settled in Paterson, New Jersey, and there found a lucrative job at six dollars per week in one of the weaving mills of the town. Six whole dollars per week was, no doubt, a fortune for Italy, but not enough to breathe on in the new country. He loved his little home. He was a good husband and devoted father to his *bambina* Bianca, whom he adored. He worked and worked for a number of years. He actually managed to save one hundred dollars out of his six dollars per week.

Bresci had an ideal. Foolish, I know, for a workingman to have an ideal—the Anarchist paper published in Paterson, *La Questione Sociale*.

Every week, though tired from work, he would help to set up the paper. Until later hours he would assist, and when the little pioneer had exhausted all resources and his comrades were in despair, Bresci brought cheer and hope, one hundred dollars, the entire savings of years. That would keep the paper afloat.

In his native land people were starving. The crops had been poor, and the peasants saw themselves face to face with famine. They appealed to their good King

Umberto; he would help. And he did. The wives of the peasants who had gone to the palace of the King, held up in mute silence their emaciated infants. Surely that would move him. And then the soldiers fired and killed those poor fools.

Bresci, at work in the weaving mill at Paterson, read of the horrible massacre. His mental eye beheld the defenceless women and innocent infants of his native land, slaughtered right before the good King. His soul recoiled in horror. At night he heard the groans of the wounded. Some may have been his comrades, his own flesh. Why, why these foul murders?

The little meeting of the Italian Anarchist group in Paterson ended almost in a fight. Bresci had demanded his hundred dollars. His comrades begged, implored him to give them a respite. The paper would go down if they were to return him his loan. But Bresci insisted on its return.

How cruel and stupid is ignorance. Bresci got the money, but lost the good will, the confidence of his comrades. They would have nothing more to do with one whose greed was greater than his ideals.

On the twenty-ninth of July, 1900, King Umberto was shot at Monzo. The young Italian weaver of Paterson, Gaetano Bresci, had taken the life of the good King.

Paterson was placed under police surveillance, everyone known as an Anarchist hounded and perse-cuted, and the act of Bresci ascribed to the teachings of Anarchism. As if the teachings of Anarchism in its extremest form could equal the force of those slain women and infants, who had pilgrimed to the King for aid. As if any spoken word, ever so eloquent, could burn into a human soul with such white heat as the lifeblood trickling drop by drop from those dying forms. The ordinary man is rarely moved either by word or deed; and those whose social kinship is the greatest living force need no appeal to respond—even as does steel to the magnet—to the wrongs and horrors of society.

If a social theory is a strong factor inducing acts of political violence, how are we to account for the recent violent outbreaks in India, where Anarchism has hardly been born. More than any other old philosophy, Hindu teachings have exalted passive resistance, the drifting of life, the Nirvana, as the highest spiritual ideal. Yet the social unrest in India is daily growing, and has only recently resulted in an act of political violence, the killing of Sir Curzon Wyllie by the Hindu Madar Sol Dhingra.

If such a phenomenon can occur in a country socially and individually permeated for centuries with the spirit of passivity, can one question the tremendous, revolutionizing effect on human character exerted by great social iniquities? Can one doubt the logic, the justice of these words:

> Repression, tyranny, and indiscriminate punishment of innocent men have been the watchwords of the government of the alien domination in India ever since we began the commercial boycott of English goods.

The tiger qualities of the British are much in evidence now in India. They think that by the strength of the sword they will keep down India! It is this arrogance that has brought about the bomb, and the more they tyrannize over a helpless and unarmed people, the more terrorism will grow. We may deprecate terrorism as outlandish and foreign to our culture, but it is inevitable as long as this tyranny continues, for it is not the terrorists that are to be blamed, but the tyrants who are responsible for it. It is the only resource for a helpless and unarmed people when brought to the verge of despair. It is never criminal on their part. The crime lies with the tyrant.[4]

Even conservative scientists are beginning to realize that heredity is not the sole factor moulding human character. Climate, food, occupation; nay, color, light, and sound must be considered in the study of human psychology.

If that be true, how much more correct is the contention that great social abuses will and must influence different minds and temperaments in a different way. And how utterly fallacious the stereotyped notion that the teachings of Anarchism, or certain exponents of these teachings, are responsible for the acts of political violence.

Anarchism, more than any other social theory, values human life above things. All Anarchists agree with Tolstoy in this fundamental truth: if the production of any commodity necessitates the sacrifice of human life, society should do without that commodity, but it can not do without that life. That, however, nowise indicates that Anarchism teaches submission. How can it, when it knows that all suffering, all misery, all ills, result from the evil of submission?

Has not some American ancestor said, many years ago, that resistance to tyranny is obedience to God? And he was not an Anarchist even. It would say that resistance to tyranny is man's highest ideal. So long as tyranny exists, in whatever form, man's deepest aspiration must resist it as inevitably as man must breathe.

Compared with the wholesale violence of capital and government, political acts of violence are but a drop in the ocean. That so few resist is the strongest proof how terrible must be the conflict between their souls and unbearable social iniquities.

High strung, like a violin string, they weep and moan for life, so relentless, so cruel, so terribly inhuman. In a desperate moment the string breaks. Untuned ears hear nothing but discord. But those who feel the agonized cry understand its harmony; they hear in it the fulfillment of the most compelling moment of human nature.

Such is the psychology of political violence.

---

1 A revolutionist committing an act of political violence.

2 *Paris and the Social Revolution.*

3 From a pamphlet issued by the Freedom Group of London.

4 *The Free Hindustan.*

WHAT WE DID ABOUT THE
SLAUGHTER AT HOMESTEAD*

It was May 1892. News from Pittsburgh announced that trouble had broken out between the Carnegie Steel Company and its employees organized in the Amalgamated Association of Iron and Steel Workers. It was one of the biggest and most efficient labour bodies of the country, consisting mostly of Americans, men of decision and grit, who would assert their rights. The Carnegie Company, on the other hand, was a powerful corporation, known as a hard master. It was particularly significant that Andrew Carnegie, its president, had temporarily turned over the entire management to the company's chairman, Henry Clay Frick, a man known for his enmity to labour. Frick was also the owner of extensive cokefields, where unions were prohibited and the workers were ruled with an iron hand.

---

* While not precisely an early writing, this extract from *Living My Life*, 83–95, recounts some of Goldman's earliest views on political violence and the propaganda of the deed. The title given here is borrowed from Alix Kates Shulman, ed., *Red Emma Speaks: An Emma Goldman Reader* (New York: Humanity Books, 1998), 280.

The high tariff on imported steel had greatly boomed the American steel industry. The Carnegie Company had practically a monopoly of it and enjoyed unprecedented prosperity. Its largest mills were in Homestead, near Pittsburgh, where thousands of workers were employed, their tasks requiring long training and high skill. Wages were arranged between the company and the union, according to a sliding scale based on the prevailing market price of steel products. The current agreement was about to expire, and the workers presented a new wage schedule, calling for an increase because of the higher market prices and enlarged output of the mills.

The philanthropic Andrew Carnegie conveniently retired to his castle in Scotland, and Frick took full charge of the situation. He declared that henceforth the sliding scale would be abolished. The company would make no more agreements with the Amalgamated Association; it would itself determine the wages to be paid. In fact, he would not recognize the union at all. He would not treat with the employees collectively, as before. He would close the mills, and the men might consider themselves discharged. Thereafter they would have to apply for work individually, and the pay would be arranged with every worker separately. Frick curtly refused the peace advances of the workers' organization, declaring that there was "nothing to arbitrate." Presently the mills were closed. "Not a strike, but a lockout," Frick announced. It was an open declaration of war.

Feeling ran high in Homestead and vicinity. The

Emma Goldman

sympathy of the entire country was with the men. Even the most conservative part of the press condemned Frick for his arbitrary and drastic methods. They charged him with deliberately provoking a crisis that might assume national proportions, in view of the great numbers of men locked out by Frick's action, and the probable effect upon affiliated unions and on related industries.

Labour throughout the country was aroused. The steel-workers declared that they were ready to take up the challenge of Frick: they would insist on their right to organize and to deal collectively with their employers. Their tone was manly, ringing with the spirit of their rebellious forebears of the Revolutionary War.

Far away from the scene of the impending struggle, in our little ice-cream parlour in the city of Worcester, we eagerly followed developments. To us it sounded the awakening of the American worker, the long-awaited day of his resurrection. The native toiler had risen, he was beginning to feel his mighty strength, he was determined to break the chains that had held him in bondage so long, we thought. Our hearts were fired with admiration for the men of Homestead.

We continued our daily work, waiting on customers, frying pancakes, serving tea and ice-cream; but our thoughts were in Homestead, with the brave steel-workers. We became so absorbed in the news that we would not permit ourselves enough time even for sleep. At daybreak one of the boys would be off to get the first editions of the papers. We saturated ourselves with the events in Homestead to the exclusion of everything else. Entire nights we would sit up discussing the various phases of the situation, almost engulfed by the possibilities of the gigantic struggle.

One afternoon a customer came in for an ice-cream, while I was alone in the store. As I set the dish down before him, I caught the large headlines of his paper: "LATEST DEVELOPMENTS IN HOMESTEAD—FAMILIES OF STRIKERS EVICTED FROM THE COMPANY HOUSES—WOMAN IN CONFINEMENT CARRIED OUT INTO THE STREET BY SHERIFFS." I read over the man's shoulder Frick's dictum to the workers: he would rather see them dead than concede to their demands, and he threatened to import Pinkerton detectives. The brutal bluntness of the account, the inhumanity of Frick towards the evicted mother, inflamed my mind. Indignation swept my whole being. I heard the man at the table ask: "Are you sick, young lady? Can I do anything for you?" "Yes, you can let me have your paper," I blurted out. "You won't have to pay me for the ice-cream. But I must ask you to leave. I must close the store." The man looked at me as if I had gone crazy.

I locked up the store and ran full speed the three blocks to our little flat. It was Homestead, not Russia; I knew it now. We belonged in Homestead. The boys, resting for the evening shift, sat up as I rushed into the room, newspaper clutched in my hand. "What has happened, Emma? You look terrible!" I could not speak. I handed them the paper.

Sasha was the first on his feet. "Homestead!" he exclaimed. "I must go to Homestead!" I flung my arms around him, crying out his name. I, too, would go. "We must go tonight," he said; "the great moment has come at last!" Being internationalists, he added, it mattered not to us where the blow was struck by the workers; we must be with them. We must bring them our great message and help them see that it was not only for the moment that they must strike, but for all time, for a free life, for anarchism. Russia had many heroic men and women, but who was there in America? Yes, we must go to Homestead, tonight!

I had never heard Sasha so eloquent. He seemed to have grown in stature. He looked strong and defiant, an inner light on his face making him beautiful, as he had never appeared to me before.

We immediately went to our landlord and informed him of our decision to leave. He replied that we were mad; we were doing so well, we were on the way to fortune. If we would hold out to the end of the summer, we would be able to clear at least a thousand dollars. But he argued in vain—we were not to be moved. We invented the story that a very dear relative was in a dying condition, and that therefore we must depart. We would turn the store over to him; all we wanted was the evening's receipts. We would remain until closing-hours, leave everything in order, and give him the keys.

That evening we were especially busy. We had never before had so many customers. By one o'clock we had sold out everything. Our receipts were seventy-five dollars. We left on an early morning train.

On the way we discussed our immediate plans. First of all, we would print a manifesto to the steel-workers. We would have to find somebody to translate it into English, as we were still unable to express our thoughts correctly in that tongue. We would have the German and English texts printed in New York and take them with us to Pittsburgh. With the help of the German comrades there, meetings could be organized for me to address. Fedya was to remain in New York till further developments.

From the station we went straight to the flat of Mollock, an Austrian comrade we had met in the *Autonomie* group. He was a baker who worked at night; but Peppie, his wife, with her two children was at home. We were sure she could put us up.

She was surprised to see the three of us march in, bag and baggage, but she made us welcome, fed us, and suggested that we go to bed. But we had other things to do.

Sasha and I went in search of Claus Timmermann, an ardent German anarchist we knew. He had considerable poetic talent and wrote forceful propaganda. In fact, he had been the editor of an anarchist paper in St. Louis before coming to New York. He was a likable fellow and entirely trustworthy, though a considerable drinker. We felt that Claus was the only person we could safely draw into our plan. He caught our spirit at once. The manifesto was written that afternoon. It was a flaming call to the men of Homestead to throw off the yoke of capitalism, to use their present struggle as a stepping-stone to the destruction of the wage system, and to continue towards social revolution and anarchism.

A few days after our return to New York the news was flashed across the country of the slaughter of steel-workers by Pinkertons. Frick had fortified the Homestead mills, built a high fence around them. Then, in the dead of night, a barge packed with strike-breakers, under protection of heavily armed Pinkerton thugs, quietly stole up the Monongahela River. The steel-men had learned of Frick's move. They stationed themselves along the shore, determined to drive back Frick's hirelings. When the barge got within range, the Pinkertons had opened fire, without warning, killing a number of Homestead men on the shore, among them a little boy, and wounding scores of others.

The wanton murders aroused even the daily papers. Several came out in strong editorials, severely criticizing Frick. He had gone too far; he had added fuel to the fire in the labour ranks and would have himself to blame for any desperate acts that might come.

We were stunned. We saw at once that the time for our manifesto had passed. Words had lost their meaning in the face of the innocent blood spilled on the banks of the Monongahela. Intuitively each felt what was surging in the heart of the others. Sasha broke the silence. "Frick is the responsible factor in this crime," he said; "he must be made to stand the consequences." It was the psychological moment for an *Attentat*; the whole country was aroused, everybody was considering Frick the perpetrator of a coldblooded murder. A blow aimed at Frick would re-echo in the poorest hovel, would call the attention of the whole world to the real cause behind the Homestead struggle. It would also strike terror in the enemy's ranks and make them realize that the proletariat of America had its avengers.

Sasha had never made bombs before, but Most's *Science of Revolutionary Warfare* was a good text-book. He would procure dynamite from a comrade he knew on Staten Island. He had waited for this sublime moment to serve the Cause, to give his life for the people. He would go to Pittsburgh.

"We will go with you!" Fedya and I cried together. But Sasha would not listen to it. He insisted that it was unnecessary and criminal to waste three lives on one man.

We sat down, Sasha between us, holding our hands. In a quiet and even tone he began to unfold to us his plan. He would perfect a time regulator for the bomb that would enable him to kill Frick, yet save himself. Not because he wanted to escape. No; he wanted to live long enough to justify his act in court, so that the American people might know that he was not a criminal, but an idealist.

"I will kill Frick," Sasha said, "and of course I shall be condemned to death. I will die proudly in the assurance that I gave my life for the people. But I will die by my own hand, like Lingg. Never will I permit our enemies to kill me."

I hung on his lips. His clarity, his calmness and force, the sacred fire of his ideal, enthralled me, held me spell-bound. Turning to me, he continued in his deep voice. I was the born speaker, the propagandist, he said. I could do a great deal for his act. I could articulate its meaning to the workers. I could explain that he had had no per-sonal grievance against Frick, that as a human being Frick was no less to him than anyone else. Frick was the symbol of wealth and power, of the injustice and wrong of the capitalistic class, as well as personally responsi-ble for the shedding of the workers' blood. Sasha's act would be directed against Frick, not as a man, but as the enemy of labour. Surely I must see how important it was that I remain behind to plead the meaning of his deed and its message throughout the country.

Every word he said beat upon my brain like a sledge-hammer. The longer he talked, the more conscious I became of the terrible fact that he had no need of me in his last great hour. The realization swept away every-thing else—message, Cause, duty, propaganda. What meaning could these things have compared with the force that had made Sasha flesh of my flesh and blood of my blood from the moment that I had heard his voice and felt the grip of his hand at our first meeting? Had our three years together shown him so little of my soul that he could tell me calmly to go on living after he had been blown to pieces or strangled to death? Is not true love—not ordinary love, but the love that longs to share to the uttermost with the beloved—is it not more compelling than aught else? Those Russians had known it, Jessie Helfmann and Sophia Perovskaya; they had gone with their men in life and in death. I could do no less.

"I will go with you, Sasha," I cried; "I must go with you! I know that as a woman I can be of help. I could gain access to Frick easier than you. I could pave the way for your act. Besides, I simply must go with you. Do you understand, Sasha?"

We had a feverish week. Sasha's experiments took place at night when everybody was asleep. While Sasha worked, I kept watch. I lived in dread every moment for Sasha, for our friends in the flat, the children, and the rest of the tenants. What if anything should go wrong—but, then, did not the end justify the means? Our end was the sacred cause of the oppressed and exploited people. It was for them that we were going to give our lives. What if a few should have to perish?—the many would be made free and could live in beauty and in comfort. Yes, the end in this case justified the means.

After we had paid our fare from Worcester to New York we had about sixty dollars left. Twenty had already been used up since our arrival. The material Sasha bought for the bomb had cost a good deal and we still had another week in New York. Besides, I needed a dress and shoes, which, together with the fare to Pittsburgh, would amount to fifty dollars. I realized with a start that we required a large sum of money. I knew no one who could give us so much; besides, I could never tell him the purpose. After days of canvassing in the scorching July heat I succeeded in collecting twenty-five dollars. Sasha finished his preparatory work and went to Staten Island to test the bomb. When he returned, I could tell by his expression that something terrible had happened. I learned soon enough; the bomb had not gone off.

Sasha said it was due either to the wrong chemical directions or to the dampness of the dynamite. The second bomb, having been made from the same material, would most likely also fail. A week's work and anxiety and forty precious dollars wasted! What now? We had no time for lamentations or regrets; we had to act quickly.

Johann Most, of course. He was the logical person to go to. He had constantly propagated the doctrine of individual acts; every one of his articles and speeches was a direct call to the *Tat*. He would be glad to learn that someone in America had come forward at last to commit a heroic act. Most was certainly aware of the heinous crime of Frick: the *Freiheit* had pointed him out as the responsible person. Most would help.

Sasha resented the suggestion. He said it had been evident from Most's behaviour since his release from Blackwell's Island that he wanted nothing more to do with us. He was too bitter over our affiliation with the Group *Autonomie*. I knew Sasha was right. While Most was in the penitentiary, I had written repeatedly to him, but he never replied. Since he had come out, he had not asked to see me. I knew he was living with Helen, that she was with child; and I had no right to break in on their life. Yes, Sasha was right, the gulf had grown too wide.

I recalled that Peukert and one of his friends had been given charge of a small legacy recently left by a comrade. Among the latter's effects a paper was found authorizing Peukert to use the money and a gun for propaganda purposes. I had known the man and I was sure he would have approved of our plan. And Peukert? He was not, like Most, an outspoken champion of individual revolutionary deeds, but he could not fail to see the significance of an act against Frick. He would surely want to help. It would be a wonderful opportunity for him to silence for ever the current suspicions and doubts about him.

I sought him out the following evening. He refused his aid point-blank. He could not give me the money, much less the gun, he declared, unless he knew for whom and for what. I struggled against the disclosure, but, fearing that all might be lost if I failed to get the money, I finally told him it was for an act on the life of Frick, though I did not mention who was to commit the act. He agreed that such a deed would prove of propagandistic value; but he said that he would have to consult the other members of his group before he could give me what I asked. I could not consent to having so many people know about the plan. They would be sure to spread the news, and it would get to the ears of the press. More than these considerations was the distinct feeling that Peukert did not want to have anything to do with the matter. It bore out my first impression of the man: he was not made of the stuff of heroes or martyrs.

I did not have to tell the boys of my failure. It was written on my face. Sasha said that the act must be carried out, no matter how we got the money. It was now clear that the two of us would not be able to go. I would have to listen to his plea and let him go alone. He reiterated his faith in me and in my strength and assured me of the great joy I had given him when I insisted upon going with him to Pittsburgh. "But," he said, "we are too poor. Poverty is always a deciding factor in our actions. Besides, we are merely dividing our labours, each doing what he is best fitted for." He was not an agitator; that was my field, and it would be my task to interpret his act to the people. I cried out against his arguments, though I felt their force. We had no money. I knew that he would go in any event; nothing would stop him, of that I was certain.

Our whole fortune consisted of fifteen dollars. That would take Sasha to Pittsburgh, buy some necessaries, and still leave him a dollar for the first day's food and lodging. Our Allegheny comrades Nold and Bauer, whom Sasha meant to look up, would give him hospitality for a few days until I could raise more money. Sasha had decided not to confide his mission to them; there was no need for it, he felt, and it was never advisable for too many people to be taken into conspiratorial plans. He would require at least another twenty dollars for a gun and a suit of clothes. He might be able to buy the weapon cheap at some pawnshop. I had no idea where I could get the money, but I knew that I would find it somehow.

Those with whom we were staying were told that Sasha would leave that evening, but the motive for his departure was not revealed. There was a simple farewell supper, everyone joked and laughed, and I joined in the gaiety. I strove to be jolly to cheer Sasha, but it was laughter that masked suppressed sobs. Later we accompanied Sasha to the Baltimore and Ohio Station. Our friends kept in the distance, while Sasha and I paced the platform, our hearts too full for speech.

The conductor drawled out: "All aboard!" I clung to Sasha. He was on the train, while I stood on the lower step. His face bent low to mine, his hand holding me, he whispered: "My sailor girl," (his pet name for me), "comrade, you will be with me to the last. You will proclaim that I gave what was dearest to me for an ideal, for the great suffering people."

The train moved. Sasha loosened my hold, gently helping me to jump off the step. I ran after the vanishing train, waving and calling to him: "Sasha, Sashenka!" The steaming monster disappeared round the bend and I stood glued, straining after it, my arms outstretched for the precious life that was being snatched away from me.

———

I woke up with a very clear idea of how I could raise the money for Sasha. I would go on the street. I lay wondering how such a notion could have come to me. I recollected Dostoyevsky's *Crime and Punishment*, which had made a profound impression on me, especially the character of Sonya, Marmeladov's daughter. She had become a prostitute in order to support her little brothers and sisters and to relieve her consumptive stepmother of worry. I visioned Sonya as she lay on her cot, face to the wall, her shoulders twitching. I could almost feel the same way. Sensitive Sonya could sell her body; why not I? My cause was greater than hers. It was Sasha—his great deed—the people. But should I be able to do it, to go with strange men—for money? The thought revolted me. I buried my face in the pillow to shut out the light. "Weakling, coward," an inner voice said. "Sasha is giving his life, and you shrink from giving your body, miserable coward!" It took me several hours to gain control of myself. When I got out of bed my mind was made up.

My main concern now was whether I could make myself attractive enough to men who seek out girls on the street. I stepped over to the mirror to inspect my body. I looked tired, but my complexion was good. I should need no make-up. My curly blond hair showed off well with my blue eyes. Too large in the hips for my age, I thought; I was just twenty-three. Well, I came from Jewish stock. Besides, I would wear a corset and I should look taller in high heels (I had never worn either before).

Corsets, slippers with high heels, dainty underwear— where should I get money for it all? I had a white linen dress, trimmed with Caucasian embroidery. I could get some soft flesh-coloured material and sew the underwear myself. I knew the stores on Grand Street carried cheap goods.

I dressed hurriedly and went in search of the servant in the apartment who had shown a liking for me, and she lent me five dollars without any question. I started off to make my purchases. When I returned, I locked myself in my room. I would see no one. I was busy preparing my outfit and thinking of Sasha. What would he say? Would he approve? Yes, I was sure he would. He had always insisted that the end justified the means, that the true revolutionist will not shrink from anything to serve the Cause.

Saturday evening, July 16, 1892, I walked up and down Fourteenth Street, one of the long procession of girls I had so often seen plying their trade. I felt no nervousness at first, but when I looked at the passing men and saw their vulgar glances and their manner of approaching the women, my heart sank. I wanted to take flight, run back to my room, tear off my cheap finery, and scrub myself clean. But a voice kept on ringing in my ears: "You must hold out; Sasha—his act—everything will be lost if you fail."

I continued my tramp, but something stronger than my reason would compel me to increase my pace the moment a man came near me. One of them was rather insistent, and I fled. By eleven o'clock I was utterly exhausted. My feet hurt from the high heels, my head throbbed. I was close to tears from fatigue and disgust with my inability to carry out what I had come to do.

I made another effort. I stood on the corner of

Fourteenth Street and Fourth Avenue, near the bank building. The first man that invited me—I would go with him, I had decided. A tall, distinguished looking person, well dressed, came close. "Let's have a drink, little girl," he said. His hair was white, he appeared to be about sixty, but his face was ruddy. "All right," I replied. He took my arm and led me to a wine house on Union Square which Most had often frequented with me. "Not here!" I almost screamed; "please, not here." I led him to the back entrance of a saloon on Thirteenth Street and Third Avenue. I had once been there in the afternoon for a glass of beer. It had been clean and quiet then.

That night it was crowded, and with difficulty we secured a table. The man ordered drinks. My throat felt parched and I asked for a large glass of beer. Neither of us spoke. I was conscious of the man's scrutiny of my face and body. I felt myself growing resentful. Presently he asked: "You're a novice in the business, aren't you?" "Yes, this is my first time—but how did you know?" "I watched you as you passed me," he replied. He told me that he had noticed my haunted expression and my increased pace the moment a man came near me. He understood then that I was inexperienced; whatever might have been the reason that brought me to the street, he knew it was not mere looseness or love of excitement. "But thousands of girls are driven by economic necessity," I blurted out. He looked at me in surprise. "Where did you get that stuff?" I wanted to tell him all about the social question, about my ideas, who and what I was, but I checked myself. I must not disclose my identity: it would be too dreadful if he should learn that Emma Goldman, the anarchist, had been found soliciting on Fourteenth Street. What a juicy story it would make for the press!

He said he was not interested in economic problems and did not care what the reason was for my actions. He only wanted to tell me that there was nothing in prostitution unless one had the knack for it. "You haven't got it, that's all there is to it," he assured me. He took out a ten-dollar bill and put it down before me. "Take this and go home," he said. "But why should you give me money if you don't want me to go with you?" I asked. "Well, just to cover the expenses you must have had to rig yourself out like that," he replied; "your dress is awfully nice, even if it does not go with those cheap shoes and stockings." I was too astounded for speech.

I had met two categories of men: vulgarians and idealists. The former would never have let an opportunity pass to possess a woman and they would give her no other thought save sexual desire. The idealists stoutly defended the equality of the sexes, at least in theory, but the only men among them who practiced what they preached were the Russian and Jewish radicals. This man, who had picked me up on the street and who was now with me in the back of a saloon, seemed an entirely new type. He interested me. He must be rich. But would a rich man give something for nothing? The manufacturer Garson came to my mind; he would not even give me a small raise in wages.

Perhaps this man was one of those soul-savers I had read about, people who were always cleansing New York City of vice. I asked him. He laughed and said he was not a professional busybody. If he had thought that I really wanted to be on the street, he would not have cared. "Of course, I may be entirely mistaken," he added, "but I don't mind. Just now I am convinced that you are not intended to be a streetwalker, and that even if you do succeed, you will hate it afterwards." If he were not convinced of it, he would take me for his mistress. "For always?" I cried. "There you are!" he replied; "you are scared by the mere suggestion and yet you hope to succeed on the street. You're an awfully nice kid, but you're silly, inexperienced, childish." "I was twenty-three last month," I protested, resentful of being treated like a child. "You are an old lady," he said with a grin, "but even old folks can be babes in the woods. Look at me; I'm sixty one and I often do foolish things." "Like believing in my innocence, for instance," I retorted. The simplicity of his manner pleased me. I asked for his name and address so as to be able to return his ten dollars some day. But he refused to give them to me. He loved mysteries, he said. On the street he held my hand for a moment, and then we turned in opposite directions.

That night I tossed about for hours. My sleep was restless; my dreams were of Sasha, Frick, Homestead, Fourteenth Street, and the affable stranger. Long after waking the next morning the dream pictures persisted. Then my eye caught my little purse on the table. I jumped up, opened it with trembling hands—it did contain the ten dollars! It had actually happened, then!

On Monday a short note arrived from Sasha. He had met Carl Nold and Henry Bauer, he wrote. He had set the following Saturday for his act, provided I could send some money he needed at once. He was sure I would not fail him. I was a little disappointed by the letter. Its tone was cold and perfunctory, and I wondered how the stranger would write to the woman he loved. With a start I shook myself free. It was crazy to have such thoughts when Sasha was preparing to take a life and lose his own in the attempt. How could I think of that stranger and Sasha in the same breath? I must get more money for my boy.

I would wire Helena for fifteen dollars. I had not written my dear sister for many weeks, and I hated to ask her for money, knowing how poor she was. It seemed criminal. Finally I wired her that I had been taken ill and needed fifteen dollars. I knew that nothing would prevent her from getting the money if she thought that I was ill. But a sense of shame oppressed me, as once before, in St. Petersburg, when I had deceived her.

I received the money from Helena by wire. I sent twenty dollars to Sasha and returned the five I had borrowed for my finery.

A BRIEF BIOGRAPHY

Goldman in 1906, photographed
for the Chicago Sun-Times.

Emma Goldman (1869-1940) was an anarchist thinker and revolutionary, a relentless champion of workers, women, and the anti-capitalist revolution. Imprisoned for inciting riot, blamed for the assassination of William McKinley, deported in the first Red Scare, called the Red Queen, the most dangerous woman in America, the High Priestess of Anarchy—she was one of the most prominent and feared radical thinkers of her age.

Born in the Russian Empire to a straitened Orthodox Jewish family, Goldman educated herself on the revolutionary literature of those turbulent times. She immigrated to Rochester, N.Y. at 16, where she worked ten-hour shifts as a seamstress by day and read the insurrectionary anarchist journal *Freiheit* by night, attending German socialist meetings in what time was left. She soon grew disillusioned with the inhumane conditions borne by the American worker. When four Chicago anarchists were wrongfully convicted and executed for the Haymarket affair, she left a brief, unhappy marriage, packed up her sewing machine, and moved to New York City to become a revolutionary.

On her very first day in the city, she would meet both Johann Most, the *Freiheit* editor who became a mentor-cum-rival, and Alexander Berkman, who became a lifelong companion in love, friendship, and revolution.

Goldman and Berkman, together with Modest "Fedya" Stein, the third member of their commune and ménage à trois, planned an *attentat*—a direct action, a "propaganda of the deed" designed to rouse the public to revolution—in response to the bloody repression of the Homestead steel strike. Their target was industrialist strikebreaker Henry Clay Frick. Berkman would shoot the man; Stein would dynamite his house, as a failsafe; and Goldman, who raised the money for the gun, would stay behind and furnish the propaganda to Berkman's deed.

The plot was a bust. Stein never made it to Frick's house; Frick didn't die, despite being shot twice and stabbed three times; nearby workers, far from joining in the *attentat*, wrestled Berkman to the ground; the Homestead strikers denounced the act; Stein went into hiding and Berkman was sentenced to 22 years. This failure, combined with her later experiences in Bolshevik Russia, would lead Goldman to her later, more qualified endorsement of violence as a political tactic. She never wavered, however, in her conviction that violence was a revolutionary necessity. "They were doubts, after all," writes Alix Kates Shulman, "about the methods of but not the need for revolution" (*Red Emma Speaks*, 254).

Her own arrest and year-long imprisonment soon thereafter, for giving her infamous Union Square speech (p. 7–8), cemented a nation-wide notoriety. It would be the first of many political arrests. Upon release, Goldman found herself in immediate demand on the lecture circuit, at home and abroad—celebrated, vilified, and unceasingly interviewed.

In 1901, self-avowed anarchist Leon Czolgosz shot and

fatally wounded sitting U.S. President William McKinley. Goldman and many of her milieu, despite being wholly unconnected to the plot, having assumed Czolgosz an infiltrator, were arrested and charged as accomplices.

Goldman was released after two weeks. The episode, however, as well as her refusal to condemn Czolgosz —"Poor Leon Czolgosz, your crime consisted of too sensitive a social consciousness" (p. 70)—led her to go to ground, isolated and fearful of her safety.

She emerged to campaign against the Anarchist Exclusion Act of 1903 (which would ultimately be pivotal in her own deportation), re-entering the public stage in earnest with her 1906 launch of *Mother Earth*. The anarchist monthly and its publishing wing became a platform for her broad-ranging ideas: on anarchism, Bolshevism, the women's emancipation movement, art, religion, birth control, marriage, prisons, education. Ideas she also promulgated around the country on a non-stop, decade-long speaking tour that funded the periodical, while the newly-released Berkman kept it running from New York. It was *Mother Earth* that first published her 1910 *Anarchism and Other Essays*, a collection born of her disillusionment with the spoken word as a vector for change.

Out of all of these incendiary ideas and activities, however, it was Goldman and Berkman's anti-draft activism that ultimately saw them deported. Charged with conspiracy and imprisoned for two years—during which Goldman of course agitated for better conditions with fellow political prisoner, socialist Kate Richards O'Hare—Berkman and Goldman were released in 1919, at the height of the first Red Scare. They became the most prominent targets of J. Edgar Hoover's career-making political deportations.

They arrived in Russia, along with 247 other American refugees, just as the Bolsheviks were consolidating power. Though previously a stalwart supporter of the Russian Revolution, Goldman was quickly disheartened by the new regime's inequalities, suppression of free speech, and, especially, its brutal quelling of the Kronstadt rebellion. She and Berkman left for Latvia, then Stockholm, then Berlin. Their criticism of the Soviet Union alienated them from much of their milieu.

She spent the next decade in exile, having early on parted ways with Berkman, eking out a living by writing and lecturing across Europe. When she found herself facing yet another deportation, this time from England, she entered an amicable marriage of convenience with Scottish coal miner and anarchist James Colton. Passport secure, she joined Berkman in Saint-Tropez and wrote her 1931 memoir, *Living My Life*. Its positive reviews marked a soft closure to her reputation as a truly dangerous subversive. Anarchism had lost its teeth, a distant relic in the new political landscape of rising fascism. Goldman was allowed back to the U.S. for a lecture tour, provided she speak only on the book.

On June 28, 1936, Alexander Berkman, destitute and ill,

died by suicide. The largely anarchist Spanish Revolution broke out less than a month later. "The crushing weight that was pressing down on my heart since Sasha's death," wrote Goldman upon being invited to the barricades of Barcelona, "left me as by magic." For the next four years, she would tour their collectives, edit their bulletins, answer their English-language mail, and agitate on their behalf across Europe and North America.

At 70 years old, Emma Goldman was raising funds in Canada for her comrades in Spain when she suffered a stroke and died. Finally allowed to return to the U.S., she was buried in Chicago, near the Haymarket martyrs.

For more on Emma Goldman and political violence, see:

Ferguson, Kathy E. "Discourses of Danger: Locating Emma Goldman." *Political Theory* 36, no. 5 (October 2008): 735–61.

Léa Gauthier, ed. and trans. *Il nous faut être prêts à chaque instant: Sur la violence politique*. Paris: Éditions Payot & Rivages, 2023.

Redding, Arthur. " The Dream Life of Political Violence: Georges Sorel, Emma Goldman, and the Modern Imagination." *Modernism/modernity* 2, no. 2 (April 1995): 1–16.

Shulman, Alix Kates. "Preface to Part Three," In *Red Emma Speaks: An Emma Goldman Reader*, edited by Alix Kates Shulman, 251–55. New York: Humanity Books, 1998.

For Goldman's later views on political violence, see:

Goldman, Emma. *My Disillusionment in Russia*. Garden City, NY: Doubleday, Page and Co., 1923.

Goldman, Emma. *My Further Disillusionment in Russia*. Garden City, NY: Doubleday, Page and Co., 1924.

www.ingramcontent.com/pod-product-compliance
Lightning Source LLC
Chambersburg PA
CBHW022102020426
42335CB00012B/790